```
MW01119755
```

Export Success and Industrial Linkages

Export Success and Industrial Linkages

The Case of Readymade Garments in South Asia

Shahrukh Rafi Khan

with

Diva Dhar
Mariam Navaid
Manisha Pradhananga
Farah Siddique
Ashima Singh and
Siyumii Yanthrawaduge

palgrave
macmillan

First published in 2009 by PALGRAVE MACMILLAN® in the United States - a division of St. Martin's Press LLC, 175 Fifth Avenue, New York, NY 10010.

Where this book is distributed in the UK, Europe and the rest of the world, this is by Palgrave Macmillan, a division of Macmillan Publishers Limited, registered in England, company number 785998, of Houndmills, Basingstoke, Hampshire RG21 6XS.

Palgrave Macmillan is the global academic imprint of the above companies and has companies and representatives throughout the world.

Palgrave® and Macmillan® are registered trademarks in the United States, the United Kingdom, Europe and other countries.

ISBN-13: 978-0-230-60850-4
ISBN-10: 0-230-60850-7

Library of Congress Cataloging-in-Publication Data

Khan, Shahrukh Rafi.
   Export success and industrial linkages : the case of readymade garments in South Asia / by Shahrukh Rafi Khan with Diva S. Dhar.
      p. cm.
   ISBN 978-0-230-60850-4 (alk. paper)
   1.   Clothing trade—South Asia—Case studies.   2.   Exports—South Asia—Case studies.   I. Dhar, Diva S.   II. Title.

HD9940.S642K43 2009
382'.456870954—dc22   2008043244

A catalogue record of the book is available from the British Library.

Design by Macmillan Publishing Solutions

First edition: June 2009

10 9 8 7 6 5 4 3 2 1

Printed in the United States of America.

This book is dedicated to Mount Holyoke College

Contents

List of Annexures

List of Tables

Preface

This book owes its genesis to a working paper by Hausmann and Rodrik (2003) on specialization in trade theory. The paper addressed an intriguing puzzle concerning why particular countries might choose to export particular commodities within their broad area of specialization. Thus, as they put it, within the broad readymade garment sector (RMG), why might Bangladesh specialize in producing hats and Pakistan in producing bedsheets? While the authors addressed this puzzle theoretically, interesting questions about the historical and microinstitutional field details that might complement theoretical answers remained, since economic trade theory is at a very high level of commodity aggregation. In pursuing this issue, the questions of "what" and "why" became incidental to, in our view, the more important question of "how," once we started to explore the underlying processes during fieldwork.

Shortly after reading this working paper, I moved to a visiting professor position at Mount Holyoke College, Massachusetts, and developed a seminar course "South Asian Economic Development." Course development once again exposed me to the importance of the textile industry, particularly the garment sector, in the early export successes of low-income countries. I was also impressed with the quality of the research papers presented for the course by some of my students, a couple of them on the textile industry with a focus on the garment sector. It was during this first course offering that I met the five excellent students who later collaborated with me on the country studies: Diva Dhar on India, Mariam Navaid on Pakistan, Manisha Pradhananga on Nepal, Farah Siddique on Bangladesh, and Siyumii Yanthrawaduge on Sri Lanka. A chapter on history and background and another on importer's perspectives were afterthoughts, and I worked respectively with Ashima Singh and Courtney A. Van Cleve on these.

I had developed a proposal for a field research study, but was advised by the Mount Holyoke's grants officer to first do a pilot project. Given the quality of student research and the students' enthusiasm and energy, it occurred to me that they might be the ideal research partners. They had the training, enthusiasm, country knowledge, and institutional support that more than made up for their lack of experience. I approached faculty members at the department, and they strongly supported the idea and encouraged me to apply for a faculty research grant.

The Dean of the Faculty at Mount Holyoke College, Don O'Shea, was also very encouraging and solicited a brief synopsis and budget. While the sum I asked for was modest, it was nonetheless much larger than a normal faculty research grant from the Research Committee at the college. Also, the funding solicited was for seniors, and the college did not normally fund senior research after graduation. Nonetheless, the Dean entertained the proposal and funding was secured for project fieldwork. This included air tickets to the five larger South Asian countries and modest field research expenses. The economics department at the college agreed to fund a symposium for the presentation of the country papers. The papers provided plenty of material for what has now become this book.

I would like to acknowledge in particular Don O'Shea for his flexibility and encouragement and Mount Holyoke College for financial support. I would also like to thank colleagues at the economics department for their encouragement, in particular Jens Christiansen, who has been a consistent and enthusiastic supporter, and Michael Robinson. I would also like to thank Gunseli Berik of the University of Utah for very helpful, detailed, and extensive comments, and the two anonymous reviewers of this book. This is the second book I have worked on with Anthony Wahl as an editor, and one could not ask for a better one, particularly in terms of thoughtfulness and quick feedback. I would like to thank Dawn Larder, senior administrative assistant of the economics department at Mount Holyoke College, for helping in various ways throughout the writing of this book. Finally, thanks to Diva Dhar for taking some excellent photographs during her fieldwork in India, one of which has been used for the cover.

PART I

Concepts and Background

CHAPTER 1

Research Question, Conceptual Framework, and Background

1.1. Introduction: Research Question

Neoclassical economic trade theory suggests that countries, on an aggregate level, specialize in products that are consistent with their particular advantages; this book suggests that the predictions of this theory are broadly borne out.[1] However, this theory is cast on a very aggregate level for sectors such as textiles and steel and the theory provides little guidance on *process*.[2] Thus, there is little one learns from this theory about business, structural, and institutional practices that make a particular country more successful than others even if their broad comparative advantage is similar. Similarly, one learns little about the various forms of critical linkages or partnerships, backward and forward (induced by industrial policy or spontaneous), public-private, domestic-foreign (in a value chain context), South-South, and intracluster or intrasector, that result in export success.[3] In a nutshell, with reference to products, existing trade theory focuses on the "what" while this book focuses on the "how" and in some cases addresses the "why."

Thus, this book is about adding to the literature by exploring historical, industrial, business, and institutional factors, various forms of linkages and partnerships, and industrial policy in South Asian countries (Bangladesh, India, Nepal, Pakistan, and Sri Lanka) using a case study method. The initial conditions for these countries are broadly similar, but they have had varying levels of success in exporting products that one could argue they all have a comparative advantage in. To provide insight into processes that could account for success, we explore public-private partnerships; joint ventures or other forms of collaboration driven by foreign direct investment in a value chain context; the associated technological diffusion, industrial clusters; social capital, as it pertains to business networks; and industrial policy in the form of state support for the garment sector.

For all the larger five South Asian countries we undertook to study, the readymade garment (RMG) sector was identified as the export success story based on a prior selection process.[4] This was unanticipated but fortuitous since we researched the same sector across different countries with similar historical and institutional conditions. It also meant that because of the elimination of the Multi-Fiber Arrangement (MFA) on January 1, 2005, this book turned out to be as much about industrial transition as about processes accounting for export success. In fact, one could argue that similar factors are likely to account for both and that the processes that account for export success are also likely to result in a more successful transition toward changing world trade conditions. While exploring transition was not planned, it nonetheless added a welcome dimension to the book.

The section outline for this chapter is as follows: We first very briefly review economic trade theory to provide a context for our primary research question. Next we discuss the literature on global value chains, within which partnerships between foreign investors and local producers are often located. This is followed by a discussion of other themes such as industrial policy, industrial clusters, social capital and collective action, and public-private partnerships that are associated with our research question. We turn next to our research design and product selection. Most of our business respondents saw their performance in a comparative South Asian context. In the last section of this chapter, we provide background information for a comparison with numbers on the socioeconomic conditions as a general frame of reference and on the business environment as a specific frame of reference.[5]

1.2. Trade Theory

It is impossible to do justice to economic trade theory in a few pages, given that separate semester courses on this theory are taught at the intermediate, advanced, and graduate levels in economics departments.[6] However, we have a very limited objective here and that is to expose the general reader to how economic trade theory relates to our research question.[7]

Classical trade theory was formalized as the theory of absolute advantage by Smith (1973), who reasoned using a two-country, two-good (commodity) framework that trade between two countries would be welfare enhancing when they specialize in producing goods that they had an absolute advantage in producing in terms of labor productivity. Thus, if the United States was more productive at producing machinery and India at producing

RMGs, both countries would be better off if the United States specialized in producing machinery and India in producing RMGs, and they traded with each other, much as individuals in a market economy specialize in one activity and buy products resulting from activities engaged in by others.

Ricardo (1962) extended the theory of absolute advantage into the counterintuitive theory of comparative advantage by demonstrating that trade between two countries, such as that in the example above, would be welfare enhancing even when one country had a labor productivity advantage in producing both goods. This theory suggests that even if the United States had an absolute advantage in producing both machinery and RMGs, specialization and trade would still make both countries better off. In this case, the United States should specialize in the product it had a greater edge in or India in the product in which the comparative disadvantage was lower.

Neoclassical theory both extended and changed the theory of comparative advantage by allowing for more than one factor of production, that is, labor was no longer the only factor. One of the most important changes was that with more than one factor, complete specialization was no longer a prediction of the model.[8] While this prediction of nonspecialization, such that a country was not predicted to produce only one of the two goods in a two-good model, was more realistic, several of the assumptions of neoclassical theory were very restrictive.[9] Some of the less important ones were easily relaxed, and so the model was generalized to more than two countries and two products that the initial theoretical developments relied on. The need to relax the more restrictive assumptions set the stage for future innovations in trade theory.

One of the most significant developments in trade theory was based on the contributions of Heckscher (1919) and Ohlin (1933), who developed it in terms of the amount of the various factors (labor, capital, land) that went into creating a product. Thus the Heckscher-Ohlin (HO) model, still cast in a neoclassical mold, is also referred to as the factor endowment model. It demonstrates the intuitive result that trade would be welfare enhancing when countries specialized in goods that are intensive in the use of factors they have in greater abundance. This theory was also generalized to the multiple good and country cases, and extensions of the theory explored the impact of trade on factor incomes (those accruing to labor and capital or businesses) within the trading partners. However, this theory too relied on other very stringent assumptions, including identical technologies and tastes across trading partners.

Trade theory evolved to explain paradoxes and anomalies in the HO model.[10] A logical expectation was that a capital-abundant country like the USA would export more capital-intensive goods, but this seemed not to be the case when the theory was tested post–World War II.[11] This paradox was partially resolved by a finer classification of factors of production, including skilled and unskilled labor, relative to the simple aggregation of factors into labor and capital.

The anomaly that focused the attention of many trade theorists was that most of world trade was between high-income nations with similar factor endowments (about two-thirds). To account for trade between similar high-income countries called for a relaxation of the more stringent assumptions of trade theory. These extensions more realistically allowed for products, tastes, and technologies to vary across countries in explaining intra-high-income or intra-industry trade.[12] Linder's (1961) explanation for trade between high-income countries was based on overlapping demand (that countries are more likely to trade with countries with similar quality preferences and hence income levels).

Vernon's (1966) product cycle theory relaxed the assumption of identical technology. Thus, a high-income country's export of a product is based on invention and innovation, but as the product reaches the mass production stage in its life cycle, the first mover might end up importing the product after having lost competitive advantage to imitators with the technology becoming nonproprietary and diffused.

Grubel and Lloyd (1975) recognized the importance of product differentiation and so relaxed the assumption of homogeneous products. Different brands of the same product, say automobiles (like Volkswagen and Ford), are traded between high-income countries. To realize economies of scale (lower cost per unit resulting from a larger scale of operation), high-income countries cater to majority taste in their own countries, but this may serve minority preferences in a high-income trading partner and hence explains trade.[13]

There are several branches of heterodox trade theory relevant to our research question. While the new-trade theory literature focuses on intra-high-income country trade, alternative heterodox models explored trade between high-income countries (North) and low-income countries (South) that was rigged to provide more benefits to the richer North based on its initial advantages in producing manufactured goods in terms of higher factor endowments and associated advantages.[14] This was referred to as cumulative causation by Myrdal (1957). Prebish (1950) referred to other advantages possessed by the North, including high-income responsiveness for Northern products, low-price responsiveness of Southern products, technological change displacing Southern products, and greater market power of Northern companies.[15]

Marxist scholars also indicated an exploitative trade association between high- and low-income countries, but one premised on the Marxist notion of extraction and transfer of surplus from low- to high-income countries. The mechanism for the transfer of surplus was demonstrated by Emmanuel (1972) using Marxian analytical tools. Marx showed that surplus flowed from where the organic composition of capital (capital-labor ratio) was low to where it was high, when explaining how values created in producing commodities are transformed into prices, and Emmanuel extended this to a cross-country setting, such that surplus flowed from low-income countries to high-income countries.[16]

The heterodox perspective most low-income countries are prone to follow is referred to as "dynamic comparative advantage." This perspective has not been elaborately developed as an elegant theory but follows from the practice of newly industrialized countries like Japan, Korea, and Taiwan. Following from this practice, low-income countries have resisted trade specialization prescriptions based on static comparative advantage (i.e., one that exists at a point in time). This is because they believe that such choices would limit their economic growth possibilities; even though they might not have static comparative advantage in some sophisticated industrial products, learning and gaining by doing possibilities (dynamic efficiencies of industrialization) and a consequent higher economic growth trajectory justify an alternative selection.[17] This perspective is very critical to the choices made by low-income countries to industrialize and move up the value chain, such as to garment from yarn production in the textile industry, and therefore is also central to the debates and case studies in this book.[18]

More recently, Grossman and Rossi-Hansberg (2006) have suggested that the nature of trade is changing from an exclusive focus on trade in goods, true in Ricardo's day, to a modern trade in "tasks" in the form of "off-shoring."[19] The latter has been enabled by the revolution in information and communication technologies, so that instructions and monitoring are possible long distances for routine tasks. Labor thus no longer competes in the production of goods but rather in performing tasks. This, they argue, has shifted the focus of attention to tasks from goods, firms, and sectors. Multinational firms can therefore retain competitive advantage by shifting tasks to where the unit costs of performing them are the lowest.[20] Grossman and Rossi-Hansberg (2006) have formalized this process, and the focus is mainly on changes in factor incomes. They disaggregate the overall effect into a terms-of-trade effect (lower prices), labor displacement effect, and a counterintuitive productivity effect, such that the average productivity on tasks still performed in high-income countries will be higher and this could have a positive impact on wages. While this analysis is novel, its key insights can be traced to Ricardo's model, which implicitly recognizes that the movement of goods and the movement of factors are substitutes, and the information and communication revolution has enabled the coordinated movement of capital and oversight as a substitute for the movement of goods. International business economists, sociologists, political scientists, and geographers turned their attention to this supply, production, commodity, or value chain analysis in the early 1990s, with a focus on governance of the chain.

This global value chain analysis, entailing the geographic distribution of tasks, is part of the conceptual framework that drove our fieldwork, and so the next section is devoted to a review of this literature. To sum up this section, we conclude that for the most part, the current revealed strength in the garment sector in South Asia is consistent with the factor endowment model. Even so, we recognize that mainstream trade theory prescription pertains to a situation that exists at a point in time and that many of the insights of heterodox theory are relevant in the evolving trade specializations in low-income countries and in the trade relations between low- and high-income countries.

1.3. Global Value Chains

Much has been written on various kinds of global value chains (GVC).[21] Raikes et al. (2000) trace the origin of value chain analysis to Wallerstein's (1974) world systems theory. They point out that prominent among the recent contributors to this analytical approach is Gereffi, who has written extensively on GVCs.[22] Gerriffi (2000, pp. 11–12) defines a global value chain to include a whole range of related activities involved in the design, production, and marketing of a product. Gereffi (1998, p. 40) refers to them as rooted in transnational production systems that link economic activities of the firms to technological, organizational, and institutional networks utilized to develop, manufacture, and market specific commodities. More relevant to this work is his explanation of GVC in terms of the location of the various nodes of control in the chain and the system of governance across them.[23]

Gereffi (1998, p. 42) provides a useful classification of the major characteristics of value chains.[24] These characteristics include source of capital, core competencies, barriers to entry, economic sectors, type of industry, ownership, type of network (investment or trade based), and structure of network (vertical or horizontal). He also distinguishes between producer chains, where the lead firm based in a high-income country has production capacity in the commodity in question but outsources as needed to a network of component suppliers based in low- or middle-income countries, and buyer-driven chains, where the lead firm does not retain production capacity but its core competencies include the high value-added functions of research and development, design, and marketing. Lead firms have the ability of creating and sustaining "brands" that create the major part of the value and draw on suppliers based mostly in low-income countries. The commonality in both chains is that the lead firm assumes the governance function, but the buyer-driven chains are the ones relevant to the RMG sector, with some of the lead firms including Gap, H&M and American Eagle.

The governance functions are required for timely delivery in the garment business, given that six to eight buying seasons are successfully delivered on for the year. In addition, various kinds of standards including managerial (for quality control) and social and environmental (to secure and maintain a good image that "sells" to share holders and customers) need to be imposed on producers. Schmitz (2006, p. 548) reports on the classification of governance in these chains into modular or captive networks.[25] Modular networks are based on the lead (apex) firm providing the design and product specifications but leaving the rest to suppliers that can be trusted to deliver as required.[26] The alternative is captive networks that also characterize producer-driven chains, in which there is much greater hands-on control of product and processes and of inspections,[27] possibly by intermediary buying agents, to ensure quality control.[28]

Given the great involvement of the lead firms in production and process, we view these corporations as a repository of valuable information. Our focus is on identifying the constraints that limit transactions and the creation of total value generated by the chain.[29] We also explore the nature of the partnership and the governance mechanisms employed to attain desired results.

1.4. Associated Themes Explaining Export Success

While the focus of the five case studies in this book is on the microlevel decision making of the firms, these agents operate in a meso and macro environment that is likely to impinge on their decision making in a trade context.[30] On a very broad level, export success could hinge on a number of factors.[31] These could include availability of natural and other resources such as capital, skilled and educated labor, a dedicated and efficient economic bureaucracy, and an entrepreneurial tradition. Export incentives could be created by the government's efforts to encourage exports with specific incentives via industrial policy.[32] Sometimes these incentives can be quite specific and their continuation premised on successfully breaking into export markets. In this case, the government can be viewed as a prime mover that might even cultivate a particular business group for the purpose.[33]

Whereas domestic factors might be central, foreign factors of various kinds also play a role both at the micro level and more broadly. This could be for strategic political reasons, whereby a high-income country provides an ally more favorable access to its markets. Taking the cue, private investment may look more favorably to investing and creating trade partnerships with an ally. The political alliance could be cemented by trade and investment links, and also private capital may view the political risk to be lower. The specific mechanisms for trade links vary, and one vehicle is outsourcing production or including the country in question as part of an international supply or production chain (section 1.3). Alternatively, bullish international demand may create export opportunities.

Our concern is with processes inducing a particular entrepreneur to break into export markets and then drawing others into production.[34] History could play a role in the choice of a particular product.[35] For example, a small town in Pakistan called Sialkot became home to a surgical-instruments-making cluster that is very successfully exporting to the West.[36] Given that the Punjab bore the burnt of many invasions, manufactured weapons had a market. The blacksmiths of Sialkot specialized in producing swords and daggers for the Mughal emperors and transitioned in the late nineteenth century to repairing surgical instruments for the American Mission Hospital. Encouraged by the hospital, the craftsmen started producing replicas of original instruments provided to them. By 1920, Sialkot was producing surgical instruments for the rest of the subcontinent, and during World War II, supplied Britain and its allies.

After the initiation and diffusion of industrial technology that leads to successful exports, there are several factors that have a bearing on sustained success. One such factor is policy—whether it helps or hinders the process, and what could be done to overcome any governmental hindrance . On the one hand, perhaps until the economic bureaucracy becomes more efficient and honest, it may be best for the government to step aside. It is quite possible, and indeed likely, that export successes were despite policy rather than because of it. Thus, in the trade theory context, it is useful to explore De Soto's (2000) proposition that overregulation constrains entrepreneurial effort and successes sometimes occur despite these constraints. He used the example of housing in the informal sector and demonstrated that in Peru, building a house on state-owned land and getting the title took 11 years, 207 administrative steps, and a visit to 52 government offices. In some cases, 728 steps were involved. Similarly, to establish a business, it took 289 days, with the prospective entrepreneur spending about six hours a day. The cost of the legal registration was about 31 times the monthly minimum wage (p. 18). The World Bank's *World Development Report 2002*

(2003, pp. 137–138) endorsed De Sota's proposition and cited other research supporting it.

On the other hand, there are several examples of public-private partnerships in the trade context where the state has in general facilitated export success or interceded on behalf of exporters with importing governments to ensure continued exports. In Pakistan, policy was able to facilitate exports in the face of foreign governments, institutions, and markets imposing standards on surgical goods (quality) and sports goods (social standards). The Pakistan government negotiated with foreign governments on behalf of industry and assured them of quality control and compliance with standards, and also it conveyed foreign buyers' and foreign governments' concerns to local producers and facilitated the meeting of requisite standards.[37]

On a broader level, this has been the case with East Asian economies like Japan, Taiwan, and Korea where exports were systematically encouraged as part of industrial policy. Hausmann and Rodrik (2003) point out that the government's efforts in Japan to engender industrialization on its own bore little fruit. It was when private initiative engaged in technology adaptations that things took off. The government created the conditions for private initiative to catch on. There was a public goods element here, because private initiative on its own would not venture where uncertainty and capital needs were too high.

Local-foreign partnerships can also catalyze an industry. Cases in point are the textile partnership between Desh, Bangladesh, and Daewoo, Korea, and the partnership in surgical goods between industrial clusters of Tuttlingen, Germany, and Sialkot, Pakistan. Daewoo (a Korean *chaebol* founded in 1967) confronted a garment quota constraint in the export market. It was also looking for markets for machinery.[38] Desh was managed by a prominent industrialist with solid government contacts. Desh and Daewoo signed a five-year collaboration agreement (rather than a joint venture proposed by Daewoo) under which Daewoo provided training in Korea for Desh workers with follow-up training in Bangladesh. Desh paid fees and royalties for marketing and consulting advice. Management, production, and marketing skills and knowledge were rapidly diffused via trained workers (also see chapter 3).

The annual average growth of garment exports from Bangladesh between 1980–1981 and 1986–1987 was 106.2 percent. Employment rose from none to 250,000, and 90 percent of those employed were women. By 2002, garments accounted for 70 percent of overseas exports, and by 2004, employment was 2 million in the garment industry and 15 million in associated industries. Garment sector's manufactured exports increased from nil to $700 million in 1985. So much so that import quotas were imposed by the USA on Bangladesh for import surges and market disruptions for several items in which it outcompeted Taiwan and Korea.[39]

When the Pakistani industrial cluster in surgical goods production started emerging as a low-cost threat to the German industrial cluster in Tuttlingen that had been dominating the market, the latter successfully diffused the threat by forging joint ventures with firms in the Sialkot cluster.[40] In the 1980s, German companies sent metallurgical engineers to train partner firms on production, engineering, and quality control, and Sialkot workers were also trained in Tuttlingen. There are regular follow-up visits to Sialkot by German technical, advisory, and inspection teams. Initially the joint venture meant outsourcing job processing to Sialkot and finishing, packaging, and marketing of the product in Germany. As metal forging improved in Sialkot and rejection rates reduced from 7 to 3 percent (1% in large firms) via cooperation with local agents of large buyers in the USA, many firms exported independently, and some even went into original brand manufacturing (OBM). Export sales from Sialkot were about 20 percent of the world trade in surgical goods at the turn of the twenty-first century. Among the factors that account for a dynamic industrial cluster in Sialkot is the intense rivalry and competition among the firms, but also the social capital–based networking and the joint action and cooperation emanating from that activity that reinforces the social capital.[41]

We rely on the case study method to explore how the conceptual framework from trade theory and the associated themes of value chains, industrial policy, industrial clusters, public-private partnerships, and social capital and collective action play out in South Asia in explaining success in garment exports. The next section explains how we conducted these case studies.

1.5. Research Design, Method, and Database

The research method called on the researchers to explore the key research question and associated themes using interviews based on a set of open-ended questions.[42] The field researchers were instructed to complete transcribing one interview before proceeding to the next to avoid contamination. These transcripts represented the qualitative database. Iarossi (2006) was used as a training tool to discuss and develop interview and field strategies. The units of analysis were senior management of exporting firms, industrial association leaders, buying agents, senior economic bureaucrats, and relevant personnel in importing firms in the United States.

One or two commodities that represented export successes over the last decade were identified for each of the five larger South Asian countries

(Bangladesh, India, Nepal, Pakistan, and Sri Lanka) using the UN online COMTRADE (Commodity Trade) data set and UN TRAINS.[43]

Stratified random sampling from sampling frames procured from, say, the Chambers of Industry or Ministry of Commerce would have been ideal. However, we anticipated that such sampling frames may not be available. The alternative plan was to secure interviews based on contacts that the researchers could muster in each country in a form of snowball sampling, and that is indeed how the field research unfolded. In practice, procuring the interviews was extremely challenging.

Prior to the fieldwork, a format for the country case studies was arrived at after discussion. The introductions describe product selection issues unique to the country based on the fieldwork. Following this, the sector background issues are discussed and the historical origin of the selected product(s) explained. The third section includes the main findings based on the research questions and interviews. While we started with an identical format for each country case study, in practice departures from the format were inevitable because identical information was simply not available for each country, and country specificities led to variations in details.

While using the case study method and relying on local researchers to explore trade success appear to replicate Porter's (1990) monumental study, this is a different and also a much more modest research endeavor. Thus, rather than exploring the broad competitive advantage of nations, albeit low-income ones, our focus is on understanding the processes that explain export success for particular products within the factor-endowment and value-chain frameworks.

1.6. Industry and Product Selection

The criteria used to identify industry and product success were based on both growth rates and the weight of the industry/product in total exports. Trading off growth relative to weight was based on judgment; for example, when the two indicators were not consistent, the choice of successful industry/product was based on judgment.[44] Based on the phenomenal success of the RMG sector within the textile industry, we decided to narrow the focus from industry to sector. Table 1.1 shows the importance of RMG sector in the country context.

During product selection, Nepal met the criteria of success identified above, but the numbers naturally did not show the negative impact of the phase out of the MFA. We retained the selected product in the sample since both success and failure provide policy lessons. The final product selection is reported in Table 1.2.

Table 1.1   RMG as a percentage of total exports in South Asia

Country	Base and terminal years	RMG as a % of total exports in base year	RMG as a % of total exports in terminal year	Rank of RMG in terminal year exports
Bangladesh	(1984, 2005)	8.5	74.7	1
Nepal	(1993, 2004)	30.8	11.1	1
India	(1988, 2005)	7.8	5.3	3
Pakistan	(1990, 2003)	13.6	20.1*	3
Sri Lanka	(1990, 2005)	23.3	26.3	1

* Number is provisional for 2003–2004.
Source: UN online COMTRADE data set, and for Pakistan, Government of Pakistan (2004, p. 101).

Table 1.2   Product selection within the RMG sector by country

Country	Product	Base and terminal year	Product as a % of total RMG exports in base year	Product as a % of total RMG exports in terminal year
Bangladesh	Men's, boys' shirts of cotton, not knit	(1989, 2004)	14.62	6.74*
Nepal	RMG sector	NA	NA	NA
India	Women's, girls' blouses & shirts of cotton, not knit/Men's, boys' shirts of cotton, not knit	(1988, 2005)	24.7/21.8	18.7/12.6
Pakistan#	Knitted cotton, men's/boys' shirts	(1990, 2003)	0.48	24.28
Sri Lanka	Women's, girls' trousers, shorts, not knit	(1990, 2005)	1.22	8.5

* The selected commodity, men's, boys' shirts of cotton, not knit, experienced rapid growth between 1998–2004. However, since the total volume of RMG exports experienced an even more rapid increase, our calculations show a lower terminal-year value for the selected commodity.
# Equivalent data for Pakistan were not present in the COMTRADE online database. *Foreign Trade Statistics* published annually by the Pakistan Federal Bureau of Statistics, at the seven-digit level from 1990–2000 and at the eight-digit level for the fiscal year 2002–2003, were used instead.
Source: UN online COMTRADE data set, Government of Pakistan (2004).

Table 1.3 Interviews by country and respondent type

Country	Senior company managers	Senior government officials	Buying agents	Industry association leaders
Bangladesh	15	0	0	2
Nepal	7	0	0	0
India	15	7	1	3
Pakistan	10	3	3	10*
Sri Lanka	11	0	2	3

For Pakistan, several of the managers were also industry-association leaders.
* Senior company managers were also representatives of various industry associations.
Source: Project fieldwork.

As Table 1.2 shows, not only was the same sector (RMG) identified as the key export success, but also within that sector, the same product (shirts) proved to be uniformly dominant across South Asia. Once again, this proved to be fortuitous for comparative analysis. However, during the fieldwork, it became difficult to focus on just that product because many units produced several products as a deliberate diversification strategy. The selected product however was used for procuring interviews.

Table 1.3 indicates the interviews procured by country for the three categories of target respondents. The list of interviewees is annexed to the country case studies except for Bangladesh.

1.7. Comparative Social, Economic, and Business Environment in South Asia and China

Our respondents invariably made reference to conditions they confronted compared to other South Asian countries they were competing with or with China. As a frame of reference, we present cross-country comparisons on social and economic indicators and, more important, on business conditions in Tables 1.4–1.6. We also provide corresponding information about China, which is currently dominating as an RMG exporter by several criteria (refer to section 2.5), as another standard for comparison. Even so, since each country chapter is designed to be self-contained, some of this information is repeated from the country perspective using alternative sources.

Sri Lanka has the best overall record on social indicators with Bangladesh sharing the honors for the lowest unemployment rate and Pakistan for the lowest inequality. The lowest ranking on other indicators varies across the other four countries. Military expenditure is included only to indicate the possibilities for social indicators if it was curbed. Pakistan does worst in this regard and Bangladesh the best.

Table 1.4 Comparative social data for South Asia and China

Variable	Bangladesh	India	Nepal	Pakistan	Sri Lanka	China
Life expectancy at birth (female, years, 2004)	64.3	64.3	62.7	65.7	77.1	73.3
Life expectancy at birth (male, years, 2004)	62.6	62.7	61.8	64.1	71.8	69.7
Mortality rate (infant, per 1,000 live births, 2004)	56.4	61.6	58.6	80.2	12.0	26.0
Mortality rate (< 5 per 1000 live births, 2004)	77	85.2	76.2	100.8	14.1	31.0
Literacy (female, % 15 years and above, 2004)	NA	47.8	34.9	36.0	89.1	86.5
Literacy (male, % 15 years and above, 2004)	NA	73.4	62.7	63.0	92.3	95.1
Unemployment (% of female labor force, 2000)	3.3	4.1	NA	16.4*	14.7[&]	NA
Unemployment (% of male labor force, 2000)	3.2	4.4	NA	6.2*	6.2[&]	NA
Poverty (headcount, % at $1 per day, PPP, 2000)	36.0	36.0	24.1@	17.0*	5.8*	16.6+
Poverty (headcount, % at $2 per day, PPP, 2000)	82.8	81.3	65.3@	73.6*	41.4*	46.7+
Poverty gap (as % of poverty line at $1 per day, PPP)	8.1	8.6	5.4@	3.1*	0.7*	3.9+
Poverty gap (as % of poverty line at $2 per day, PPP)	36.3	36.1	26.8@	26.1*	12.1*	18.4+
GINI Index (2002)	31.8^	NA	47.2@	30.6	40.2	44.7+
Military expenditure (% of GDP, 2005)	1.1	2.9	2.0	3.4	2.7	2.0

@ Data for 2004.
& Data for 2003.
* Data for 2002.
+ Data for 2001.
^ Data for 2000.
Source: World Bank, World Development Indicators.

Table 1.5   Comparative economic data for South Asia and China

Variable	Bangladesh	India	Nepal	Pakistan	Sri Lanka	China
Per capita GDP (constant US$2000, 2005)	415.3	586.5	232.2	595.6	1,004.1	1,444.8
Inflation, consumer prices (%, 2005)	3.2@	4.3	2.8@	9.1	11.6	1.8
Exports of goods and services (% of GDP, 2005)	16.1	18.9@	16.1	15.3	34.0	33.9@
FDI, net inflow (% of GDP, 2004)	0.79	0.77	0.26&	1.16	1.16	2.84
Electric power consumption (kWh per capita, 2003)	127.7	435.3	67.9	407.8	325.1	1378.5
GDP per unit energy use (constant 2000 PPP$ per kg oil equivalent, 2003)	10.8	5.2	4.03	4.2	8.8	4.5
Mobile phone subscribers (per 1,000, 2004)	31.0	43.8	6.7	33.0	113.8	258.3
R&D (% GDP, 2002)	0.62	0.85^	0.66	0.22	0.14^	1.44@
Paved roads (% of total, 2003)	9.5@	62.6*	53.9	60.0	81.0	79.9

@ Data for 2004.
& Data for 2003.
* Data for 2002.
^ Data for 2000.
Source: World Bank, World Development Indicators.

We turn next, in Table 1.5, to economic indicators that represent the broader context for business conditions.

Table 1.5, not surprisingly, suggests that economic indicators are associated with social indicators. Thus, in most cases, Sri Lanka dominates, though not in macroeconomic management, as it had the highest inflation rate in 2005. Nepal showed the poorest economic indicators, although it has the lowest inflation rate. India showed the best effort with regards to Research and Development (R&D) and Sri Lanka the worst, as a percentage of GDP.

Industrialists in our country case studies invariably made reference to the low industrial productivity and the poor business environment they had to cope with relative to their competitors in the other South Asian countries or China. To provide context and set the record straight upfront in this regard, we provide comparative data, in Table 1.6, on business conditions at roughly the time South Asian countries were engaging in competition for a larger market, post the MFA phase out.

Table 1.6 Comparative data on business conditions in South Asia and China

Variable	Bangladesh	India	Nepal	Pakistan	Sri Lanka	China
% of managers surveyed ranking this as a major business constraint (2003)						
Corruption	57.9	37.4	NA	40.4	16.9	27.3
No confidence in courts	82.9	29.4	NA	62.6	31.2	17.6
Finance	45.7	19.2	NA	40.1	20.4	22.3
Electricity	73.2	28.9	41.7	32.9	41.3	29.7
Dealing with officials	4.6	15.3	NA	10.6	NA	19.0
Tax rates	35.8	27.9	NA	45.6	19.1	36.8
Labor regulations^	10.8	16.7	NA	15.0	25.6	20.7
Labor skills	19.8	12.5	NA	12.8	21.3	30.7
Policy uncertainty	45.4	20.9	NA	40.1	34.0	32.9
Time required to (days, 2005)						
Build a warehouse	185	270	147	218	164	363
Enforce a contract	365	425	350	395	440	241
Register property	363	67	2	49	63	32
Start business	35	71	21	24	50	48
Resolve insolvency	4	10	5	3	2	2
Pay taxes (hours)	640	264	408	560	NA	584
Procedures needed for (nos., 2005)						
Build a warehouse	13	20	12	12	18	30
Enforce contract	29	40	28	46	17	25
Register property	11	6	2	5	8	3
Business startup	8	11	7	11	8	13
Other business conditions (2005)						
Cost of business start-up (% GDP)	81.4	53.0	69.9	18.6	10.4	13.6
Telephone faults per 100 mainlines	NA	126*	78#	NA	6.8#	NA
Total credit to the private sector (% of GDP)	31.7	41.1	30.7	28.4	31.6	114.9
Lender interest rate	14.0	10.8	8.1	NA	7.0	5.6
Risk premium on loans	NA	NA	5.9	NA	−2.03	NA
Business taxes (% of gross profits)	50.4	43.2	31.8	57.4	49.4	46.9
Taxes on international trade (% of revenue)	32.6@	13.8@	16.0	13.6	11.9*	−8.4#
Financial information infrastructure (index: 0 low, to 10 high)	NA	5.5	3.5	5.0	4.0	5.5

@ Data for 2004.
# Data for 2003.
* Data for 2002.
^ Refer to Table 5.6 for Nepal.
Source: World Bank, World Development Indicators.

No South Asian country dominates the rest across the board in terms of superior business conditions. Sri Lanka and India have the least bad conditions on several alternative counts, while Bangladesh generally presents the most constraints. However, there are exceptions, and Sri Lanka poses the most constraints with regards to labor regulations and Bangladesh the least with regards to dealing with officials and labor regulations. But these are subjective perceptions of managers, and their expectations can vary across countries. Thus, caution is needed in the interpretation of the numbers, and 21.3 percent of the managers in Sri Lanka, the South Asian country with the highest literacy rate, viewing labor skills as a constraint may simply mean much higher expectations since the basics are taken for granted.

Apart from dealing with officials being viewed as a constraint, the second and third set of variables could be viewed as the amount of red tape businesses have to confront. In this regard, Bangladesh and India need to do the most work, and Nepal appears to have engaged in the most deregulation in reducing red tape. Other business conditions vary: the financial information infrastructure is best for India as is the total credit forwarded to the private sector as a percent of GDP, and the interest rate and cost of business start up is lowest for Sri Lanka. Pakistan rates lowest in terms of the burden of business taxes (57 percent of gross profits) and Nepal the highest. Overall, Sri Lanka has the most favorable environment for business, Bangladesh the worst. Nepal is the most deregulated.[45]

These findings are confirmed using an alternative source as reported in Table 1.7.

Table 1.7 Procedural trade hurdles faced by South Asian countries and East Asia and the Pacific

Country/Region	Documents for export (number)	Signatures for export (number)	Time for export (days)	Documents for import (number)	Signatures for import (number)	Time for import (days)
Bangladesh	7	15	35	16	38	57
India	10	22	36	15	27	43
Nepal	7	12	44	10	24	38
Pakistan	8	10	33	12	15	39
Sri Lanka	8	10	25	13	15	27
South Asia	8.1	12.1	33.7	12.8	24	46.5
East Asia and the Pacific	7.1	7.2	25.8	10.3	9	28.6

Source: Wickramsinghe. (2006, pp. 14–15); cited World Bank data.

Once again, businesses in Bangladesh, followed by those in India, face the most constraints, and businesses in Sri Lanka, followed by those in Pakistan, the least. We use Tables 1.4–1.7 as a backdrop for the country case studies in Part II of the book.

Summary

Economic trade theory suggests that countries, on an aggregate level, specialize in products that are consistent with their particular advantages. However, this theory is cast on a very aggregate level and provides little guidance regarding the processes that might make one particular country, relative to another, successful in exporting similar products even if they share similar comparative advantages and other initial conditions. This book explores historical, industrial, business, structural, institutional, policy, and global processes in five of the larger South Asian countries to account for how and why some of them have had more export success than others. Our concern is with entrepreneurs who were able to break into particular export markets and thereby draw others into the production and also with how there may be a diversification into related products. This entails understanding the initiation and diffusion of industrial technology that leads to successful exports and also the processes referred to above that provide the supportive state and business environment.

Our research method is based on researchers from the countries in question engaging in field interviews based on a set of questions drawn from our conceptual framework and related themes. The units of analysis were senior management and industrial association leaders of exporting firms, buying agents, and senior economic bureaucrats responsible for the garment sector. We also attempted to interview importers in the United States, which is one of the main export markets, but this proved to be unsuccessful and we have documented the process and lessons learnt for other researchers in the Appendix.

One or two commodities that represented the most dramatic export successes over the last decade (for which data were available) were identified for each of the five larger South Asian countries (Bangladesh, India, Nepal, Pakistan, and Sri Lanka) using the UN online COMTRADE and TRAINS data sets. Success was defined in terms of growth in the last decade or so and export weight of the commodity in total exports in the terminal year. Before beginning the field research, we had not anticipated that RMGs would be identified as the success story in all cases; that this happened was fortuitous since it enabled a comparative evaluation of export success for the same sector, and for the most part the same product, across South Asia.

There are several complementary research issues that we flag in this chapter and will address in detail in the case studies, and this broadens the scope of the book. One related issue is whether policy helps or hinders the process of breaking into export markets. It is possible that export successes were despite policy rather than because of it. Thus, in the trade theory context, we will explore the proposition that overregulation constrains entrepreneurial effort and successes sometimes occur despite these constraints.

We will also explore industrial policy and its supportive role and specific examples of successful policies that can result in mutual learning in South Asia and beyond. There are also several examples of public-private partnerships in the trade context whereby the state has in general facilitated export success or negotiated with importing governments to ensure continued exports.

Local-foreign partnerships and joint ventures can also catalyze an industry and result in adoption, adaptation, and diffusion of technology, and we delve into this issue. In so doing, we investigate the nature of production or value chains that firms in the RMG sector become part of and the nature of standards that they need to comply with.

We also investigate the nature of competition and cooperation within the garment sector (cases of collective action), the nature of linkages of the sector with the broader economy, and the linkages of the sector across country within South Asia (South-South linkages).

The textile industry in general and the garment sector in particular have played an important role in all currently high- and middle-income countries starting with the Industrial Revolution. However, the textile industry flourished in the region now referred to as South Asia (then India) even prior to the Industrial Revolution. We turn briefly to a historical account of the growth of the textile industry before turning to the country case studies in Part II of this book.

Annexure 1.1

Management Research Questions

Background information

- Number of employees?
- Wage bill?
- Value of capital stock?
- Products?

— Percentage of each product exported?
— Is this firm part of an industrial cluster?

[Get copy of annual report]

[Below is a checklist of questions. You will need to probe and explore issues as they come up.]

When did you start to produce product X?

When did this sector (RMG) get started?

How did this sector get started?
[This is important, i.e., the origin]

What do you think accounts for the export success of this sector?

Do you think your firm is successful as an exporter?

If yes, why? If not, why not?

Is the government helpful in enabling your production in anyway?
[Explore partnerships]

What could the government do to be of [more] assistance?

Is the government a hindrance to your production in any way?

Do you have strong links with other firms in the sector?
[Exploring social capital]

If so, what is the basis of these links?

Have other firms in the industry helped your production in any way?

Have other firms in the industry hindered your production in any way?

Have you engaged in any joint action with firms in the sector for mutual benefit?
[Explore partnerships]

If so, what was the nature of the collective action and how was it organized?

How did you access the relevant technology?
[Explore the process of technology diffusion]

Are you confronting or have you confronted any problems in exporting from within your country and if so what are they?

Are you confronting or have you confronted any problems in exporting posed by the country you are exporting to and if so what are they?

Do you have a partnership with any foreign firms?
[Explore partnerships]

If yes, what is the nature of the partnership?

Explain the origin of the partnership.

How was the contact established?

Did you solicit the partnership or were you approached?

Has the foreign firm helped in any way with regards to the following?

- Technology?
- Management assistance?
- Quality control?
- Marketing assistance?
- Funds?
- Other?

Does this firm have a code of conduct?

- Based on social standards?
- Based on environmental standards?
- Other?

[Remember to get contacts of foreign partners and contacts of relevant persons in government]

How satisfied are you with this partnership?

What do you anticipate the future of this partnership [to be]?

Annexure 1.2

Economic Bureaucrat Research Questions

What are your goals with regards to this sector (i.e., RMG)?

What have you done to help this sector?

What are your future plans to help this sector?

[Confront them with complaints you might have heard from management]

CHAPTER 2

The Textile and Readymade Garment Industry in South Asia: A Brief History and Reemergence

2.1. Introduction

The textile industry in general and garments, as the most labor-intensive sector, have been the road taken by most countries in their path to manufacturing and industrialization.[1] This was the case with the currently high-income countries (HICs), and the trend continued with Japan and East and South East Asia. This chapter will start with a discussion of the rise of textile and clothing industries in the latter regions. Historically, as some nations lost comparative advantage due to rising unit labor costs, other countries, in a flying geese pattern, assumed the competitive mantle, and these have more recently included China, Vietnam, and Cambodia.[2] The second section of this chapter briefly narrates this changing pattern of comparative advantage.

South Asian countries including Bangladesh, India, Pakistan, and Sri Lanka have also become competitive players in the world export market for textiles and clothing. While India and Pakistan have played an active role as major exporters of textiles, the prominence of the RMG sector is relatively recent, and this sector has benefited from the availability of quotas available under the MFA (see section 2.5 of this chapter). Even so, the textile industry has a long history in the subcontinent.[3] The third section of this chapter investigates the role that the main actors, the spinners, weavers, and traders, initially played in India in establishing comparative advantage in the textile industry as producers and marketers of raw materials and cheap cloth. The role of the East India Company and the impact of colonialism are discussed as limiting the growth of India's textile industry. The fourth section explains how this continued to be the case right up to India's independence in the mid-twentieth century. The final section of the chapter documents the emergence of the RMG sector in South Asia in the fourth quarter of the twentieth century, the sector's significance, and how it is withstanding the initial years of the MFA phaseout.

2.2. The Textile Industry in East and South East Asia

Saxonhouse (2005, p. 431) documents how, during the Meiji period, Japan began exporting cotton yarn produced with imported machinery primarily to China as well as other parts of East Asia. As early as 1894, industrial policy in the form of subsidies and the lifting of duties on exports and raw cotton imports was used to encourage production. Due to the lack of a natural resource base, Japan chose to industrialize by expanding its manufacturing capabilities. The flying geese metaphor (see endnote 2 of this chapter) has also been applied by Ozawa (2005) to shifting production patterns within a country, specifically Japan. Thus, starting at the end of the nineteenth century, Japan first imported raw cotton, after which it engaged in import substitution for domestic production of fibers, followed by aggressive export promotion that generated a trade surplus.

Meyanathan and Ahmed (1994, p. 5) document that the first half of the twentieth century was the period in which Japan reached its peak in cotton-based exports. With technological progress and changing comparative advantage over time, it began to focus on the more capital-intensive techniques in the production of textiles and apparel. In the 1950s and 1960s, the newly industrialized countries (NICs)[4] became less costly sites of production for light manufactures (Anderson 1994, p. 89). This pattern is evident from the data reported in Table 2.1.

Table 2.1 shows that textile and clothing exports from Japan accelerated at the end of the nineteenth century and reached a peak of 36 percent of total exports in the 1950s. The contribution of this industry to total GDP and employment grew concomitantly, although the peak was reached earlier, in 1920s for employment and in 1930s for GDP. This reflects the shift to higher-value capital-intensive production in the 1920s and hence the continued higher contribution to GDP until the 1930s, after which Japan diversified into other goods and this industry became less important in terms of contribution to employment and GDP. In the 1920s, while this industry's contribution to total manufacturing and employment declined, its contribution to total manufactured exports and to total GDP share of manufacturing continued to rise.

After Japan, South Korea was among the NIEs that made a foray into garment production in Asia.[5] Smith (1996) documents this process indicating how conglomerates, referred to as chaebols, facilitated the organization of

Table 2.1 The economic significance of textiles and clothing in Japan, 1874–1987 (percentages)

Year	Textiles and clothing's share in total				Textiles and clothing's share in manufacturing		
	GDP@	Employment	Exports	Imports	GDP@	Employment	Exports
1874–1879	NA	NA	4	54	10#	NA	25
1880–1889	2	NA	9	44	18	NA	36
1890–1899	4	NA	23	19	26	NA	51
1900–1909	5	7	28	11	26	62	51
1910–1919	7	8	34	8	28	61	52
1920–1929	8	9	34	5	30	55	56
1930–1939	9	6	35	3	28	37	54
1950–1959	3	4	36	0	11	22	38
1960–1969	2	3	19	1	7	14	19
1970–1979	1	2	6	3	5	11	6
1980–1985	1	2	4	3	4	8	4
1985–1987	NA	NA	3	3	NA	NA	3

NA: not available.

@ Gross domestic product shares in the prewar period are at constant 1934–1936 prices, thereafter at current prices.

The interpretation, for example, is that of manufacturing's total contribution to GDP; the share of textile and clothing was 10 percent in 1874–1879.

Source: United Nations, *Yearbook of National Accounts Statistics*, New York, various issues; International Labor Organization, *Yearbook of Labor Statistics*, various issues; Bank of Japan, *Economic Statistics Annual*; Ohkawa and Shinohara (1979) and Yamazawa and Yamamoto (1979) as cited in Anderson (1994).

the RMG sector. Orders for garments from the international markets were placed with the chaebols, who then subcontracted the production to small-sized enterprises. South Korea acquired the reputation of being one of the leading exporters of high-quality apparel, and, between 1967 and 1980, the clothing exports achieved a record growth rate of nearly 60 percent.

Smith also documents how, following the Japanese trajectory, the industry suffered a setback as South Korea faced labor shortages and hence rising wages; this contributed to the shift from garment production to capital-intensive fabrication of textiles, which would then be exported to cheaper and lower-skilled garment-producing nations like Indonesia (pp. 224–225).[6] Korean chaebols also began to look for offshore sites in which they would have a controlling investment and through transfer of technology and know-how could produce garments for export. These sites were in countries where labor was abundant and wages were therefore much lower, and which had not exhausted their export quotas to markets in HICs under the MFA (see section 1.8).[7]

Thus, the original Asian NIEs including South Korea, Taiwan (China), and Hong Kong made investments in cheaper locations when domestic production proved too expensive. In Indonesia, the industry took off after 1979 following the devaluation of the Indonesian rupee. Smith (1996, p. 228) reports that garment exports increased from $14 million in 1979 to $6.1 billion by 1993. Industrial policy pursued by the government, including the lifting of duties on imports for garment exporters, helped in the expansion of production. Hill (1994, p. 149) documents how garment production, as the most labor-intensive sector, initiated the textile industry.

Smith (1996) explores Vietnam as his second case study and shows how it followed the same route to industrialization a decade later; that is, via the RMG sector. The process of opening up the Vietnamese economy, also called *doi moi*, began in 1986, following which investors from more technologically advanced countries, including Korea, entered the market to take advantage of the abundant labor and the extremely low wages, almost half the daily Indonesian wage at that time. To begin with, textiles and garments were the only set of manufactured commodities in Vietnam's top ten exported goods—the rest were extractive or agricultural products.

In the post-Mao era, China also entered the world export markets in textiles and clothing in a big way. The reforms after 1978 had a tremendous impact as they opened up the economy to trade with the rest of the world. Just like the NIEs in their earlier stages of industrialization and the South East Asian economies, including Malaysia, Thailand, Indonesia, and the Philippines, in their second tier of industrialization, China too, following its reforms in 1978, relied on its plentiful labor willing to work at exceptionally low wages for its success in RMG exports. It rapidly became the cheapest mass producer of all kinds of manufactured products, of which garments constituted a significant part.

While China and other newly developing South East Asian countries like Vietnam and Cambodia continue to be important players in the RMG world market, the larger South Asian countries including Bangladesh, India, Pakistan, and Sri Lanka have also emerged as competitors consistent with the flying geese pattern. India, in fact, has a long history as a leading producer in textiles, and in the next section, we turn first to the beginnings of the textile industry in this region in the seventeenth and eighteenth centuries.

2.3. The South Asian Textile Industry in the Seventeenth and Eighteenth Centuries

Chaudhuri (1996, pp. 38–41) presents a fascinating account of the textiles as India's most important industry in the seventeenth and eighteenth centuries. What is most striking about this account is the complexity of the industry in terms of linkages across the value chain,[8] diversity, and sophistication. He points to Gujarat, Punjab, Bengal, and the Coromandel Coast as the four main areas where the textile trade has flourished since the seventeenth century.

These regions specialized in and became known for different products (p. 39), and their geography also impacted production and exports. Dacca was famous for its fine muslins, Kasimbazar (also in Bengal) for its silk goods and taffetas, towns in western and central India for "fine embroidered quilts, satins, chintz, and the famous transparent muslin *Ab-I raven* (meaning flowing water)," and the area around Masulipatnam (now in Andhra Pradesh) for "the fine varieties of painted cloth." The regional specialization in the production of different kinds of cloth and fabrics appears to be based on spatial advantages. For example, the quality of Dacca's muslin was based on the "rigid quality control" of the cotton harvested on a narrow strip of land about 40 miles long and two to three miles wide along the Meghna river (p. 72). The Masulipatnam region was probably able to produce "bright and durable colors" because of "the chemical interaction" between local water salts and the available local dyes.

Notwithstanding the regional specializations, Chaudhuri (p. 44) also points to several common characteristics that determined the comparative advantage of textile making regions alluded to above. All engaged in active interregional and foreign trade and had an enterprising business class, adequate sources of raw cotton, ample skilled labor, and the ability to generate an agricultural surplus to keep the price of wage goods low. Another tendency was agglomeration, which brought together a whole range of associated and complementary industrial skills.[9] Finally, the quality of the political governance and transportation would impact regional fortunes (p. 35).

Indian manufacturers also had the technical proficiency to cater to the consumer preferences of the particular markets they exported to, such as the Middle Eastern, South East Asian, and later Western markets. For example, a weaver supplying to Middle East buyers used techniques to starch and glaze cloth so that it appeared as smooth as paper (p. 42). Later, as textile exports to Europe increased, weavers, particularly those in Bengal, adjusted to European specifications (p. 43).

Thus, Chaudhuri (1996, p. 37) points out that long before Europe became a potential market for India's textile products, Indian weavers dominated the export of textiles to the Asian and African markets; as it was "the world's greatest producer of cotton textiles . . . the finer and luxury products were almost entirely supplied by India." India had a clear comparative advantage, even though the quality of the cloth produced in different areas could vary significantly because cotton could grow anywhere in India with the provision of water. Moreover, almost all villages had a few weavers producing cloth with qualitative differences between the products for the local market and those for the international market. This practice of product differentiation by market can be viewed as a precursor to the establishment of textiles as a principal industry.

Weavers produced textiles and clothing for local consumption, and in some cases for exports, after they received cash advances, so that they could buy raw materials and supplies. Production only for local consumption was insufficient for sustaining the livelihoods of weavers that worked in this industry throughout the year, without any supplemental income from agriculture. This was because they had difficulty selling all of their product when they began to specialize, and this specialization resulted in a surplus. However, the textile industry as a whole was able to overcome this difficulty and flourished by selling the surplus in international markets, and weavers and traders became connected through a large network of intermediaries owing to their involvement in the international markets.

Thus, the rise of textile manufacturing in these earlier centuries can primarily be attributed to India's comparative advantage over the textile industries in the West and the other parts of the world. The low cost of production due to the ample availability of raw materials and skilled workers at extremely low wages resulted in traders and merchants representing the East India Company purchasing Indian cloth to sell in Britain with high profit margins. Chaudhuri (1978, p. 16) reports that the British East India Company's total volume of trade with the Indian subcontinent at the turn of the seventeenth century increased from 73 percent of the entire trade of the company to 83 percent within two decades.

The East India Company played an important role in shaping the growth of the industry. During the first half of the eighteenth century, the British were encouraging the settling of weavers in places like Bombay, and they tried to create settlements for the growth of textiles where a certain measure of standardization and organization was possible under their control, as cloth was produced in bulk for the European market. In this they achieved a measure of success when political insecurity caused itinerant weavers to fear for their lives and livelihoods that made them settle in less vulnerable places (p. 56).

The industrial organization in Bombay closely followed the traditional "putting out" system of European guilds, where yarn and looms were supplied to weavers who settled there. Along with Bombay and Madras, the East India Company also undertook business with sites of production in Bengal. Because of the superior quality of the cloth and the availability of cheap water transportation, Bengal was an ideal location from which trade could be undertaken without unnecessary shipping costs (p. 43).

Arasaratnam (1996) documents the production structure of the hand-loom industry in Southeastern India between 1750 and 1790. The key intermediaries were the merchants who advanced the finance capital and linked the weavers to the markets. He explains that this was not like the "putting-out" system of European guilds, in that the weavers received a cash advance and not materials, and they retained control of all stages of the production process and also, in principle, of the marketing. In practice, barring obvious opportunities in a seller's market, such as playing off European buying agents against each other, they relied on the merchants.

Brokers were another key intermediary as the agents of the merchants, and they fronted the advance and also collected the product and ensured quality control. Given that they knew the business as ex-weavers and belonged to the same caste, they were part of the social network and performed a vital function. The caste village headman was also an intermediary and played the role of the overseer. While he did not impinge on the autonomy of the weavers, he could play a mediating role and received a commission for the service. The economic history of the period suggests that the weavers did little better than earn subsistence wages, not necessarily because of the intermediaries but because prosperity in the profession would draw more people into the occupation.

The cash advances paid to weavers gave them flexibility, because if the final products were rejected on the basis of poor quality, the lack of standardization, or the unwillingness of the British to pay the right price, the weavers could take their goods to the Dutch or French East India Company warehouses. This made the sale of Indian textiles to the final buyer a fairly competitive process (pp. 55–56).

However, using the case of Southeastern India, Arasaratnam (1996) explains that once the British gained political ascendency, they blocked competition. Initially, in the weaver villages they gained control of, they tried to enhance profits by cutting out the intermediaries and establishing direct contacts, via company agents accompanied by armed company personnel, with the caste headman in the village.[10] The mistaken impression was that the weavers would welcome this, since they could now potentially share the savings with the buyer. They also tried to impose the traditional "putting out" system as a measure of control. This intervention failed because it was based on a faulty understanding of the intermediary network, which the weavers actually supported, and the village headman had little control on production and he did not seek to impose it. The attempt to impinge on the weaver's production autonomy through the "putting out" system also met with robust resistance. Eventually, the resistance was worn down and the weavers were converted to wageworkers, as in the medieval European craft guilds. Control was extended to production by instituting in-kind payments (supply of materials) and via inspection of tools and payments linked to subsistence. By controlling the prices of weavers output, and suppressing their standard of living, the Company was able to maximize its profits.

Using a "world systems"[11] conceptual framework, Matson (1990) suggests that the widespread British control on Indian textile production was the real cause of the decline of the textile industry in the country that began around 1750. In this world systems core-periphery framework, Indian manufacturing, which was on the periphery, was brought into the orbit of the world capitalist system and via the transfer of surplus served Britain as part of the core i.e. the essence of the colonial extraction process. The Industrial Revolution in the latter half of the eighteenth century accelerated this process of decline of Indian textile manufacturing, which could no longer compete with the productivity of machines.[12] Thus, citing Chaudhuri, Matson reports that textile exports from India, as a percentage of total exports, declined from 52.6 percent in 1795–1800 to 3.7 percent in 1850–1881 (p. 223). Rapid technological innovation in Britain resulted in handloom spinning and weaving being replaced by machines producing cheaper cloth.[13]

The European companies and the colonialists shifted their focus from importing finished textiles to importing raw materials from India. Certain types of fabric and materials that could not be reproduced in European mills continued to be imported in large quantities, but machine production and the imposition of an asymmetric tariff structure wiped out the profitability of textile export to the West.[14] In the new world system, India would now provide the raw materials for the superior production capacity in the West (p. 207).

To sum up, this section described the growth and subsequent decline of the Indian textile industry and the role played in this process by the British, particularly the East India Company.

2.4. The Indian Textile Industry in the Nineteenth and Twentieth Century

The late nineteenth century saw the emergence of large-scale textile mills in parts of India, such as Bombay, where initially spinning yarn brought about a surge in yarn exports. This was followed by weaving mills with power-looms. Rothermund (1993, pp. 52–54) documents that in 1854, a Parsi entrepreneur, C. N. Davar, opened the first cotton textile mill in Bombay, and the industrial manufacturing of textiles began to coexist with the indigenous industry of spinning and weaving. The expansion of the industry continued with 32 cotton mills opening between 1872 and 1878 in Bombay and also other parts of the country, and this was seen as an attempt to engage in industrialization within the limits imposed by the colonial government. By 1924, one-third of the cotton textile mills existed in Bombay with other hubs being created in Ahmedabad in Gujarat, Kanpur in the North, Madras and Madurai in the South, and Solapur in the Deccan. Surprisingly, the growth of mills did not occur in eastern India and specifically in Bengal, which used to be the chief centre for the industry in earlier centuries.

Matson (1990, pp. 225–227) argues that in spite of the establishment of these textile factories, and even though mills displaced the hand spinners, the handloom labor continued. Also, even with the expansion of mills, such technological innovation did not occur that might threaten Britain's dominance. In fact, as Matson (p. 228) put it, the development of the mills too was meant to cater to the expansion of British industry, as shown by the fact that 95 percent of the looms were imported from Britain in the 1920s, and India accounted for a third of all British machinery exports, principally for textile manufacturing. Indian mills produced a coarse count yarn compared to the much finer count exported from Lancashire in Britain and hence did not pose any threat. Cloth from Lancashire accounted for 50 percent of cloth consumption in India in 1913.

Rothermund (1993, p. 54) cites two main likely constraints to the growth of an Indian indigenous capital goods industry: first, the British colonial administration would resist the necessary protective tariff for India to avoid threatening their own commercial interests; second, as is generally the case in the political economy of such decisions, downstream interests in India, that is the existing mill owners, would also have resisted the initially more expensive and lower-quality indigenously produced capital equipment. The Indian industry was thus rooted in the production of low-quality grey cloth that did not require great technological input over time and effectively made use of the factor of production and raw material that India had in abundance, that is, cheap labor and cotton (p. 53).[15] India also continued to receive finished products from Britain, which meant that the indigenous RMG sector could not flourish.

Therefore, in the first half of the twentieth century, a combination of the harmful effects of colonialism and the lack of incentives for Indian textile entrepreneurs prevented robust industrialization; neither were there backward linkages created by the indigenous producers of cloth, nor was there import substitution to enable the export of finished goods. It was not until the later part of the twentieth century that the RMG sector came into its own in South Asia as shown in the next section.

2.5. Textile and RMG Industry's Emergence in South Asia

A combination of trade rules, foreign investments, government industrial policies, and an increasing demand for low-cost garments in the West served as a catalysts for the growth of the RMG sector and a shift in focus from raw materials and textiles to apparel. Since the 1950s, the HICs, such as the United States, Canada, and various European countries, had placed some form of quantitative restrictions on the import of textiles and clothing to protect their industry. These include a Short-Term Cotton Textile Trade Agreement (STA) which transitioned into the Long-term Cotton Textile Trade Agreement (LTA) and then four phases of the MFA designed under the General Agreement on Trade and Tariffs (GATT) starting in 1974, and finally the Agreement on Textile and Clothing (ATC) negotiated under the Uruguay Round, which also formed the World Trade Organization (WTO—which incorporated the GATT and other agreements) to oversee ATC as part of its mandate.[16] These were designed to give breathing space to HIC textile industries.

Annexure 2.1 demonstrates that all South Asian countries showed a remarkable growth rate in garment exports during the protected stage of the industry. The growth ranged from a seven-fold increase for Nepal, relative to 1982, to a 38-fold increase for Sri Lanka, relative to 1979. The big success story however is Bangladesh, which demonstrated a 3,722-fold increase from a small base in 1980. A comparison with Pakistan elucidates this point. Pakistan's garment exports in 1982 were almost 13-fold higher than Bangladesh's. Within a decade, Bangladesh had virtually caught up, and by 2004 its garment exports were about double those of Pakistan's at over $6 billion.

Table 2.2 below shows the significance of the textile and garment industries at the turn of the century on the eve of the MFA phaseout for all South Asian countries but particularly Bangladesh, Pakistan, and Nepal.

Table 2.2 shows that Bangladesh, Pakistan, and Sri Lanka are all heavily reliant on textiles and clothing. A very large percentage of the textile employees in Bangladesh and Sri Lanka are women, an issue to which we will return in the case studies, and, by contrast, the percentage of female employees in the textile and clothing industry in India is surprisingly low.

The garment sector in all the South Asian countries faced increased global competition due to the MFA phaseout on January 1, 2005, agreed

Table 2.2 Contribution of textile and clothing to South Asian economies

Country	Year	Total employment ('000)	Share of [textile] manufacturing to total employment (%)	Females share in textile and clothing employment (%)
Bangladesh	2004	1,800	NA	90
India	2001	NA	22	11
Pakistan	2001	2,300	43	30
Sri Lanka	2000	237	49	87

NA: not available or not validated.
Source: UNDP (2006, Table 4.4 and Figure 4.3). Information drawn form International Labor Organization (ILO) sources.

Table 2.3 Growth in South Asian and Chinese garment exports to the United States and European markets, 2004–2007 (percentages)

Country	United States	Europe
Bangladesh	60.17	19.72
China	102.58	94.82
India	41.54	49.42
Nepal	−65.25	−16.57
Pakistan	31.94	13.11
Sri Lanka	1.98	42.15

Source: U.S. Department of Commerce and U.S. International Trade Commission, http://dataweb.usitc.gov/scripts/REPORT/asp, and Eurostat, External Trade, http://epp.eurostat.ec.europa.eu/.

to in the Uruguay Round of trade liberalization.[17] This meant the elimination of import quotas in HICs and the establishment of a freer trade regime for the industry, but also that many low-income countries, including the South Asian countries we chose to study, no longer had a guaranteed market. Thus, while the MFA phaseout meant an opportunity for those ready for it, it also meant a challenge for those not as competitive. It was widely predicted that after the MFA phaseout, many low-income country textile industries, including those in South Asia, such as Bangladesh, would not be able to withstand the competition from China and India.[18]

We explored this issue using data collected by U.S. and European statistical agencies. The detailed results are reported in Annexures 2.2 and 2.3 and the summary table drawn from them is reported as Table 2.3.[19] China's export data are also reported to explore how it fared after the phaseout of the MFA relative to the South Asian countries.

Table 2.3 shows that the prediction that China would capitalize on the freer trade regime in garments has been borne out, at least in the initial years post the MFA phaseout. Thus, China's garment exports to the U.S. and EU markets increased by 102 percent and 95 percent, respectively, between 2004 and 2007. The Chinese conceded a temporary "market disruption" clause in garments as part of their WTO accession agreement with the United States and the European Union till 2008. These have been invoked by both the United States and the European Union, so the full brunt of its export growth increase in garments may not yet have been felt by the competition.[20] South Asia may also be at a competitive disadvantage relative to Eastern Europe (for exporting to the EU) and to Mexico and the Caribbean (for exporting to the United States) that have preferential access to the respective markets and also a location advantage.[21] India's exports also showed a robust growth rate, of 42 percent and 49 percent in the U.S. and EU markets, respectively. Bangladesh and Pakistan showed an export growth of 67 percent and 32 percent respectively, in the U.S. market, and Sri Lanka a 42 percent export growth in the EU market. The prediction of market collapse has borne out for Nepal that revealed negative growth rates of 65 percent and 17 percent in the U.S. and EU markets, respectively. Sri Lanka's export growth of 2 percent in the U.S. market and Pakistan's export growth of 13 percent in the EU market are also anemic in contrast to competitor countries. While it is still too early in most cases to tell how the post-MFA competition and other market forces will play out, the decline in Nepal's garment sector seems nonreversible. This data review sets the stage for the case studies in chapters 3 to 7.

Conclusion

Following the "flying geese" model, the textile and clothing industry has been relocating to the cheapest sites of production. In the earlier part of the nineteenth and twentieth centuries, comparative advantage shifted from the West to Japan, following that to the newly industrializing countries of East Asia (Korea, Taiwan (China), Hong Kong, and Singapore), and on to emerging South East Asian economies (Malaysia, Thailand, Indonesia, and Philippines). In the current phase of this international shifting of comparative advantage and production, other South East and East Asian countries have emerged, including China, Vietnam, and Cambodia, but South Asia has also shown strength in textile and garment production.

The South Asian region's (then India) dominance in the textile industry dates back to well before the seventeenth century. Abundant skilled craftsmen and raw materials and a complex and successful production and trading network sent high-quality products to many parts of the globe including Africa, the Middle East, South East Asia, and the West. This strength was originally tapped for profit by the East India Company. Subsequently, this strength was harnessed for additional profit for the company as it imposed direct control on production, made possible by military conquest and political control. Eventually, the Industrial Revolution in Britain shifted comparative advantage, and the industry in India lost its former glory. Colonial British interests allowed a resurfacing of the industry in the nineteenth and twentieth century, but in subservience to and with protection of British commercial interests, and there was little chance that the industry in India would flourish under such circumstances.

Ironically, the South Asian region got an opportunity to lay its claim to the global trade in textiles and garment due to Western protectionism. The decimation of the Western textile industry due to the shifting comparative advantage threatened jobs, and the political response evolved into a multilateral protectionism in the form of various agreements including four rounds of the MFA under the agency of the GATT and the ATC under the WTO. This protectionism assured export quotas, based on an evolving formula, to most countries and South Asian countries were able to lay claim to these quotas. Cheap labor, favorable industrial policies, and quota hopping by more advanced developing countries that had exhausted their own quota saw the robust emergence of the textile and clothing industry in virtually all South Asian countries, particularly Bangladesh.

However, fledgling South Asian textile industries were put in a state of flux due to the phaseout of the MFA on January 1, 2005, as part of the Uruguay Round trade liberalization agreements. We engaged in a preliminary data-based examination of how the different South Asian countries coped with a more competitive global market environment for garments after the phase-out of the MFA. In keeping with predictions, the Chinese and Indian garment industries have increased their world export market dominance, but contrary to predictions, the other South Asian countries, except for the Maldives and Nepal, have held their own. Once again, Bangladesh has demonstrated robust growth despite the increased competition. Part II of the book, starting with Bangladesh, will document in detail the processes underlying the performance.

Annexure 2.1 Garment exports from South Asia to the world ($s)

	Bangladesh	India	Nepal	Pakistan	Sri Lanka
1978	NA	410,035,136	NA	NA	NA
1979	NA	536,195,904	NA	NA	70,846,296
1980	1,691,161	590,312,128	NA	NA	109,056,248
1981	4,686,455	716,789,760	NA	NA	153,147,840
1982	11,390,088	566,690,880	NA	143,492,591	165,739,328
1983	20,661,996	717,269,760	NA	226,378,376	201,551,616
1984	76,671,816	826,755,584	NA	244,471,475	293,577,120
1985	167,527,776	914,207,104	27,595,682	255,824,328	279,297,440
1986	180,254,389	1,103,905,024	44,590,876	462,994,809	323,886,976
1987	331,972,092	1,500,272,128	28,248,548	606,910,080	417,721,408
1988	474,732,371	1,571,189,888	40,716,884	623,084,032	428,272,224
1989	449,504,674	2,217,852,160	44,536,344	NA	466,248,384
1990	642,955,735	2,532,793,088	49,681,812	1,013,511,744	642,977,024
1991	840,382,730	2,531,139,840	36,703,144	1,209,189,760	790,562,258
1992	1,041,735,424	3,105,983,897	77,867,056	1,442,927,360	1,183,299,836
1993	1,307,392,063	2,976,986,880	84,926,976	1,558,230,400	1,355,960,497
1994	1,478,795,264	3,712,077,056	79,837,952	NA	1,484,050,816
1995	1,969,208,076	4,124,337,152	111,388,096	1,611,236,224	NA
1996	2,218,496,069	4,231,324,333	104,846,680	1,810,389,248	NA
1997	2,688,465,012	4,359,409,152	108,805,256	1,810,389,248	NA
1998	3,785,888,479	4,797,578,240	105,746,552	1,839,780,224	NA
1999	NA	5,170,163,544	138,405,808	1,846,284,416	2,291,773,440
2000	4,161,664,280	6,193,227,146	209,394,336	2,144,201,344	NA
2001	4,077,069,924	5,495,966,099	NA	2,136,393,781	2,440,508,832
2002	4,083,968,824	6,048,347,136	NA	2,228,419,840	2,349,511,936
2003	5,066,840,240	6,641,704,657	225,760,071	2,710,177,391	2,513,157,796
2004	6,295,713,559	6,643,257,091	NA	3,025,736,188	2,776,155,752

NA: not available.
Note: The data are based on Standard Industrial Trade Classification (SITC Rev. 2, 84) for all countries except Pakistan, which used an SITC Rev. 3., 84 classification to report the data. The two-digit number 84 stands for "articles of apparel and clothing accessories."
Source: United Nations COMTRADE data set, http://comtrade.un.org/.

Annexure 2.2 Garment exports to the United States from South Asia and China, 2004–2007 (million US$)

Country	HTS #	2004	2005	2006	2007	% change (2004–2007)
Bangladesh	61	499.24	587.40	733.90	818.70	63.99
	62	1,372.88	1,680.62	2,075.43	2,179.82	58.78
Total		1,872.12	2,268.02	2,809.33	2,998.52	60.17
China	61	4,102.98	6,576.96	8010.01	10,563.53	157.46
	62	6,617.92	10,230.96	11,857.62	13,406.83	102.58
Total		10,720.9	16,807.92	19,867.63	23,970.36	123.59
India	61	679.51	937.20	1,162.64	1,318.52	94.04
	62	1,597.52	2,121.03	2,079.53	1,904.38	19.21
Total		2,277.03	3058.23	3,242.17	3,222.9	41.54
Nepal	61	28.98	13.01	10.09	6.41	−77.88
	62	69.22	48.10	40.77	25.71	−62.86
Total		98.20	61.11	50.86	34.12	−65.25
Sri Lanka	61	451.40	589.95	712.60	706.31	56.47
	62	1,101.96	1,063.48	974.36	877.80	−20.34
Total		1,553.36	1,653.43	1,686.96	1,581.84	1.98
Pakistan	61	857.46	928.07	1,033.10	1,069.01	24.67
	62	289.75	345.15	394.37	444.64	53.46
Total		1,147.21	1,273.22	1,427.47	1,513.65	31.94

HTS: Harmonized System.
61 Articles of apparel and clothing accessories, knitted or crocheted.
62 Articles of apparel and clothing accessories, not knitted or crocheted.
Insignificant in terms of millions.
HTS 61 and HTS 62 add up to SITC 84.
Source: U.S. Department of Commerce and US International Trade Commission, http: //dataweb.usitc.gov/scripts/REPORT/asp.

Annexure 2.3 Garment exports to the European Union from South Asia and China, 2004–2007 (million Euros)

Country	HTS #	2004	2005	2006	2007	% change (2004–2007)
Bangladesh	61	1,583.88	1,648.29	2,170.61	2,120.53	33.88
	62	1,065.55	941.41	1,192.41	1,051.24	−1.34
Total		2,649.43	2,589.7	3,363.02	3,171.77	19.72
China	61	2,886.51	4,264.95	4,969.61	6,020.78	108.58
	62	5,076.34	7,221.34	8,416.78	9,492.57	87.00
Total		7962.85	11,486.29	13,386.39	15,513.35	94.82
India	61	875.94	1,078.58	1,298.97	1,336.15	52.54
	62	830.00	1,099.32	1,343.74	1,212.93	46.14
Total		1,705.94	2,177.9	2,642.71	2,549.08	49.42
Nepal	61	3.94	3.94	3.98	4.94	25.38
	62	15.99	14.10	12.39	13.34	−16.57
Total		19.93	18.04	16.37	18.28	8.28
Sri Lanka	61	146.20	151.72	207.51	253.61	73.47
	62	138.59	145.45	177.59	197.00	42.15
Total		284.79	297.17	385.1	450.61	58.73
Pakistan	61	288.34	210.81	251.96	244.30	−15.27
	62	337.39	335.32	380.31	381.62	13.11
Total		625.77	546.13	632.27	625.92	0.02

61 Articles of apparel and clothing accessories, knitted or crocheted.
62 Articles of apparel and clothing accessories, not knitted or crocheted.
Insignificant in terms of millions.
Source: Eurostat, External Trade, http://epp.eurostat.ec.europa.eu/.

PART II

Country Case Studies

CHAPTER 3

The Readymade Garment Sector in Bangladesh

3.1. Introduction

The RMG sector represents the manufacturing export success story of Bangladesh and, indeed, of South Asia (see Annexure 2.1).[1] It accounted for 3 percent of GDP in 1991, and this share dramatically increased to 13 percent by 2006.[2] This sector has occupied a dominant position among manufactured exports since 1988, when it overtook the traditionally flourishing jute exports. During 1983–1984, the RMG sector's share of total exports was 3.89 percent, whereas by 2006–2007, it had grown to 76.04 percent.[3] In 2006, the RMG sector provided direct employment for 2 million workers (about 90 percent of whom were female), and the apparel supporting industry employed 0.8 million workers.[4] This was about 3.6 percent of the total labor force.[5]

As explained in chapter 2, the global apparel and textile industry had historically been highly protected until the scheduled elimination of quantitative restrictions under the Uruguay Round Agreement on Textiles and Clothing (ATC) on January 1, 2005 (see chapter 1). Bangladesh emerged as an exporter of apparel in the global market in the 1970s as a result of the MFA's diverting orders toward smaller exporting countries.[6] When established exporters of apparel, such as Hong Kong and Korea, reached their MFA import quota ceilings, an opportunity for new entrants like Bangladesh was created. It entered the export market by engaging in collaborative arrangements involving technology transfer and investment financing with established exporters.[7] Foreign buyers also wanted to avail themselves of the cheap and unskilled/semiskilled labor that Bangladesh possessed in abundance, for completing their supply orders.[8]

Large-scale production of RMGs is a relatively new phenomenon in Bangladesh, and until the 1960s, tailors made garments according to individual customer specifications. A domestic market for RMGs was virtually nonexistent except for children's clothing and men's undershirts made of knitwear (*genji*).[9] The RMG sector started in the late 1970s as a nontraditional sector with a negligible export base, but achieved rapid growth and now occupies a prominent position in Bangladesh's exports and employment, as explained earlier. Units in the sector are privately owned and are fully export oriented, while ownership in the rest of the textile industry is equally divided between state-owned enterprises (SOEs), the majority of which suffer from inefficiency, and private mills, which are more competent producers of yarns and fabrics.[10]

In the rest of this chapter, we first briefly describe the RMG sector and its export performance and the regional focus of its exports. We turn next to the fieldwork to identify factors accounting for the success of garment exports, comment on the post-MFA scenario, and end with summary and conclusions.

3.2. The RMG Sector and Export Performance

RMG factories are located in Dhaka, Chittagong, Narayanganj, Savar, and Tongi-Gazipur.

Until the end of 1982, there were a mere 47 garment manufacturing units.[11] However, in 1984–1985, there was a spike in growth and the number of RMG factories increased to 500.[12] In 2006, the number of RMG units was estimated to be around 3,560.[13] In addition, there were 211 spinning mills, 278 weaving mills, and 115 dyeing, printing, and finishing operations.[14]

Low-cost garments such as cotton shirts and trousers characterize the majority of apparel exports. Table 3.1 shows the breakdown of the main apparel items exported from Bangladesh.

Table 3.1 indicates that trousers and T-shirts were important export items and that the export of both dramatically increased in 2005–2006 relative to 2004–2005, despite the phaseout of the MFA. Of the main export items shown in the table, only jackets demonstrate a mild decrease in export value.

Table 3.2 shows the distribution of RMG exports by major destinations. The main export destinations for Bangladesh are the European Union (EU),[15] which accounted for approximately 50 percent of total RMG exports in 2005–2006, and the United States, which accounted for approximately 34 percent of total RMG exports for the same period.[16] While Bangladesh

Table 3.1 Value of the main apparel export items from Bangladesh (million US$)

Year	Shirts	Trousers	Jackets	T-Shirts	Sweaters
1993–1994	805.34	80.56	126.85	225.90	–
1994–1995	791.20	101.23	146.83	232.24	–
1995–1996	807.66	112.02	171.73	366.36	70.41
1996–1997	759.57	230.98	309.21	391.21	196.60
1997–1998	961.13	333.28	467.19	388.50	296.29
1998–1999	1043.11	394.85	393.44	471.88	271.70
1999–2000	1021.17	484.06	439.77	563.58	325.07
2000–2001	1073.59	656.33	573.74	597.42	476.87
2001–2002	871.21	636.61	412.34	546.28	517.83
2002–2003	1019.87	643.66	464.51	642.62	578.37
2003–2004	1116.57	1334.85	364.77	1062.10	616.31
2004–2005	1053.34	1667.72	430.28	1349.71	893.12
2005–2006	1056.69	2165.25	389.52	1781.51	1044.01

Source: Bangladesh Garment Manufacturers and Exporters Association (BGMEA).

Table 3.2 Distribution of major RMG exports from Bangladesh by major destination (percentages)

Year	United States	EU	Combined share of United States and EU	Export share of other countries
2001–2002	42.67	55.43	98.10	1.90
2002–2003	38.02	57.12	95.14	4.86
2003–2004	28.64	65.42	94.06	5.94
2004–2005	30.64	64.24	94.88	5.12
2005–2006	33.67	49.77	83.44	16.57

Source: BGMEA.

lost share in its main market, the EU, it made up for this with an increased market share in the United States. Market diversification is evident: even as the combined share of the United States and EU dropped about 10 percent to 83 percent in 2005–2006, the share of other countries increased by this percentage. Asia was the major source of imported inputs, with China, India, and Korea being the major trading partners.[17] We turn now to a brief description of the fieldwork and the findings that emerged from our survey.

3.3. Fieldwork

The fieldwork was conducted in Dhaka and Chittagong during June–August 2006 and included interviews with RMG manufacturers and officials at the Bangladesh Garment Manufacturers and Exporters Association (BGMEA).[18] Informal interviews were also conducted with female workers in the RMG sector. The fieldwork in Dhaka and Chittagong was to a certain degree constrained by the labor unrest in the RMG sector in May–June 2006. It was also not possible to visit the Export Processing Zone (EPZ) in Dhaka or Chittagong due to safety concerns.

Due to problems of access, a random sample selection was not possible. Interviewees had to be selected via a process of referral based on contacts. The interviewees were generally welcoming and willingly shared their knowledge about their firms and the sector. However, they were not comfortable sharing financial information about their firms. Thus, discretion was used regarding such questions so as not to alienate the interviewee. While some interviewees readily shared information about their firm's main foreign buyers, the majority of them did not disclose any specific buyer contact information (for follow-up interviews). This is not surprising given that buyers are a closely guarded secret in a highly competitive environment, and we found the same reluctance in the other South Asian countries covered in this volume.

3.4. Findings

3.4.1. The Origins of the RMG Sector

A majority of studies on the RMG sector postulate that one of the prime reasons for its establishment was the MFA quotas that diverted production to smaller exporting countries, such as Bangladesh.[19] The conventional explanation is that MFA trade restrictions contributed to the international fragmentation of the supply chain, such that low-wage countries, such as Bangladesh, began stitching imported pre-cut materials.[20] The system of quotas penalized the more competitive suppliers such as Hong Kong and Korea and benefited less competitive suppliers located in countries that had not fully utilized export quotas and whose only competitive advantage was low unit cost, mainly due to low wages.[21]

While the aforementioned external factors were crucial in the development of the RMG sector in Bangladesh, other domestic and external factors played a similarly important role. All of the interviewees highlighted the pioneering role of Desh Garments Ltd. and its founder, Mr. Nurul Qader, in the development of the RMG sector. Prior to the arrival of Desh, smaller units such as Reaz Garments and Paris Garments had produced apparel for both domestic and export markets. However, it was Desh that introduced the concept of assembly-line production. As one interviewee noted, prior to Desh, other factories were "cottage industries" rather than export-oriented manufacturing units.[22] Desh, which was the first fully export-based nonequity joint-venture firm in the RMG sector, was established in 1979. It formed a technical and marketing collaboration with Daewoo Corporation of South Korea.[23] Desh had 120 operators (including three women) trained in South Korea in making men's shirts and started production of men's shirts in Bangladesh in 1980.[24]

Desh played a fundamental role in the process of technology diffusion in the RMG sector. Employees of Desh who had received training in Korea soon left Desh to open their own garment factories. Two of the interviewees who were former Desh employees spoke of Desh's pioneering role in the RMG sector. The interviewees reasoned that since Desh employees had received training in making men's basic shirts, it was an obvious choice for those that started their own businesses to produce men's shirts, since they already had the technological know-how and had established contacts with buyers. Also, the interviewees noted that the style for men's basic shirts is fairly simple, the machine layout does not have to be changed, and the operations have potential for substantial productivity growth. However, most manufacturers had diversified into other products as well.

The interviewees revealed that the outbreak of civil war in Sri Lanka in the early 1980s was a turning point for Bangladesh's RMG sector development, because a lot of orders were diverted to Bangladesh. Some interviewees mentioned that trained personnel from Sri Lanka came to Bangladesh to train workers.

3.4.2. Explaining Individual Success and the Success of the RMG Sector

Most of the interviewees responded affirmatively when asked if they considered themselves successful manufacturers. When asked to explain the reasons behind their success, the majority cited their hard work and dedication, their relationships with their buyers, and their flexibility in terms of catering to buyers' needs. The same story was repeated when the interviewees were asked about the reasons behind the RMG sector's success. There was a general perception among them that Bangladeshi entrepreneurs are flexible, adaptable, and responsive to buyers' needs. They also cited goodwill and established contacts with foreign buyers as other reasons for success. Some mentioned cheap labor that allows Bangladesh to offer its products at a lower price than India or China. When asked about the perceived lower productivity of Bangladeshi labor, due to either lower levels of education or other factors, the interviewees almost unanimously refuted this perception. Table 3.3 shows an intercountry comparison of productivity in the RMG sector in Bangladesh relative to other countries for 2000.

Table 3.3 Comparison of Bangladesh's productivity in the RMG sector with other countries

Country	Person minutes per basic operation
United States	14.00
Hong Kong	19.75
South Korea	20.75
Sri Lanka	24.00
Bangladesh	25.00

Source: Bhattacharya and Rahman (2000).

Table 3.4 Comparative unit price of selected apparel items exported from Bangladesh to the United States (US$ per dozen)

	2002	2003	Jan. to Oct. 2004	2002	2003	Jan. to Oct. 2004
Product type	Nonknit cotton shirts			Nonknit man-made fiber shirts		
World average	74.22	74.71	78.18	52.11	52.30	51.91
Bangladesh	53.06	50.07	50.89	55.37	50.50	45.04
China	76.60	79.99	85.92	49.62	51.13	51.62
India	59.36	64.11	71.92	47.79	56.72	68.26

Source: World Bank (2006).

While worker productivity in Bangladesh is much lower than that in the highly capital-intensive United States, it is very close to that in Sri Lanka, which is a prominent South Asian competitor, and is not too far behind the productivity in Korea, classified as a high-income country. The majority of the interviewees considered Bangladeshi workers very hardworking and adept at picking up new skills. A story often told is that Bangladeshi workers, especially women, have very agile fingers (that are required for the sewing process) because they habitually pick fish bones with their fingers.[25] One interviewee claimed that while Sri Lankan workers might have slightly higher productivity, buyers would prefer buying basic shirts from Bangladesh because the price offered on each shirt is "easily $2 cheaper" owing to the much lower wages in the country (i.e., the unit labor cost is much lower). Table 3.4 shows a comparison of the unit price of selected apparel items exported to the U.S. market.

Table 3.4 provides possible[26] support for the anecdotal evidence suggesting cheaper exports from Bangladesh. While average prices of Chinese and Indian shirts between 2002 and 2004 rose, those of shirts exported from Bangladesh fell.

3.4.3. Industrial Policies

Interviewees differed on the government's role in supporting and promoting the RMG sector. While some lauded the government's back-to-back letter of credit (L/C) scheme that allowed purchase of raw materials for export and the creation of bonded warehouses (for duty free imports), others considered the RMG lobby as having pushed for this and saw very little contribution from the government.[27] A few interviewees regarded the back-to-back L/C scheme as having come about due to the efforts of Mr. Nurul Qader, who used to be a senior civil service-officer preindependence, and hence was influential in government circles. In any case, RMG manufacturers viewed the creation of back-to-back L/C as crucial since it allowed them to get goods against a new L/C without having to first pay off the one before. This addressed the liquidity requirement of businesses. The other supportive government initiative was the creation of an export-friendly policy environment, including a stable exchange rate regime.[28]

3.4.4. Hindrances to the RMG Sector's Growth

Some interviewees strongly denied any positive contribution of the government in the sector's development. They felt that the RMG sector had developed through its own effort and hard work. Also, some RMG manufacturers thought that the government should take steps to address certain internal inefficiencies that were hindering the growth of this sector. The unstable domestic political situation came up repeatedly during conversations with RMG manufacturers. Many complained that frequent *hartals* (strikes) called by the opposition parties disrupted the production and the delivery of orders. Even though a law was passed stipulating that hartals were not to affect the RMG sector, disruption of transportation services meant that fabrics or other shipment lay idle at the port or that the owners were not able to ship the consignments. Also, the safety of RMG workers was a concern during *hartals*.[29]

Some interviewees felt that the government had failed to provide adequate protection for RMG manufacturers. They also said that the government had failed to address the minimum-wage issue prior to the labor unrest. Twelve years before the unrest in 2006, the minimum wage for RMG workers had been set at 930 taka (Tk.) by the government.[30] Following the labor unrest in the RMG sector, the government formed a wage board on May 31, 2006, and asked the board for its recommendation for a new pay scale for the workers within 90 days. The RMG factory owners accused the government of having failed to regularly adjust the minimum wage and criticized the proposed sudden, sharp hike in wages to Tk. 3,000. Owners expressed concern that if wages increased suddenly, they would not be able to absorb the extra cost.

Another problem of great concern to RMG manufacturers was the corruption that had become endemic within customs. Because of customs delays and bribes, RMG manufacturers incurred extra expenses. Some RMG manufacturers acknowledged that sometimes customs is very strict about the import of fabrics because a few unscrupulous manufacturers sell the imported (duty-free) fabric on the local market. They suggested that, perhaps, on the basis of the previous track records, "good" manufacturers could be allowed to clear customs relatively easily.

Most manufacturers noted that the existing port in Chittagong did not have sufficient capacity to meet the requirements of the RMG sector. They complained that port congestion kept their imported fabrics from reaching export markets in time and this increased their lead or delivery time. Port congestion also hampered the timely delivery of their consignments. Sea freight is vital to Bangladesh's economy as about 80 percent of the country's trade depends on it.[31] The Chittagong port handles about 85 percent of the country's total trade, and in recent years imports passing through the port have risen by 25 percent and exports by 15 percent (no breakdown is available specifically for the RMG sector imports and exports). Also, the number of feeder ships operating between Singapore and Chittagong has also risen from 29 to 47.[32] However, the port's infrastructure has not developed sufficiently to keep pace with the increased port traffic, and this has led to great additional costs as ships have to queue up for days at a time to berth and incur costs between $10,000 and $20,000 per day for sitting idle. Furthermore, feeder operators impose additional surcharge to reduce congestion loss.[33] Port congestion is one main reason why the turnaround time for global trade to and from Bangladesh is viewed by exporters as slow, and for the RMG sector the lost time is extremely damaging.

While some RMG owners suggested that the government update existing port facilities in Chittagong to cope with the greater demand, others felt that given the importance of the RMG sector to the economy, the government should build a dedicated deep-sea port for RMG trade.

Interviewees also indicated that the government needs to improve negotiating skills within the WTO, so that Bangladesh gets its due in future negotiations. Despite qualifying in per capita income terms, Bangladesh was denied least–developed-country status in the Hong Kong Ministerial in December 2005, which would have enabled it to have duty-free access to the EU and United States.[34] Bangladesh faces an average tariff of 14 percent on goods sold to the United States.[35]

3.4.5. Linkages

Linkages in the RMG sector in Bangladesh have evolved in the classic pattern identified by Hirschman (1958). The RMG sector primarily consists of woven and knit products, and in the initial stages of its growth, woven items had been the biggest contributor to export earnings. However, in the post-MFA period, the growth of woven RMG export has declined by 5.38 percent compared with the previous year (under MFA quotas). Knitwear exports have continued to increase sharply even after the MFA phaseout. The knitwear sector experienced a growth of 31.10 percent in the post-MFA period compared with the prior year (under MFA quotas).[36] In 1994, knitwear exports were valued at US$341.53 million (18 percent of total RMG exports), whereas in 2006 this figure rose to US$4,388.72 million (almost 50 percent of total RMG exports).[37]

In its initial phase, the RMG sector was heavily dependent on imported fabrics and accessories. Fabrics and accessories such as interlining, labels, buttons, and sewing thread; packaging materials like neck boards, backboards, plastic collar stays, tissue paper, hangtags, pins and clips, hangars and poly-bags, zippers and draw strings; and export cartons were all imported.[38] However, over the past decade, the phenomenal growth of the RMG sector has been accompanied by rapid growth in linkage industries supplying fabrics, yarns, accessories, and packaging materials. Currently, domestic accessories industries meet 70 percent of the RMG sector demand.[39]

While the domestic supply of accessories is thought to have kept up with the RMG sector's requirements, the domestic supply of fabrics is lagging far behind the RMG sector's demand. An estimate by the Center for Policy Dialogue (CPD) showed that the gap in the demand and supply of fabric was 2,400 million meters for the year 2000.[40] CPD estimates that in order to meet the capacity shortfall, Bangladesh would have to double its spinning, weaving, dyeing, and finishing capacity by 2010.[41]

Supporting service industries such as transportation, banking, shipping, and insurance have proliferated to keep pace with the demands of the RMG sector.[42] The indirect employment generated by the RMG sector is estimated at 200,000 workers.[43] World Bank (2006) estimates the number of people indirectly dependent on the RMG sector to be 10 million.

The domestic production of knitwear fabric grew rapidly in response to the needs of the knit RMG sector. Due to lower setup costs (in comparison with the woven sector, which is much more capital-intensive) the knitwear sector comprises integrated plants that have knit yarn and fabric processing as well as knit garment production capacity. The integrated plants are said to have expanded as a result of low investment costs, relatively simple technology, favorable European Union Generalized System of Preferences (EU GSP) facilities, and generous government cash compensation scheme (CCS—equivalent of 10 percent of value added) on exports of garments made from domestically produced fabric and yarn.[44] In contrast, in the woven sector, large investment costs have hampered the development of backward-linkage industries such as spinning and weaving, and thus woven fabric manufacturing and woven garment manufacturing remain separate activities.[45] Also, global excess capacity in the woven fabric sector kept prices of woven fabrics low and therefore limited the domestic growth of woven fabric manufacturing.[46]

Field interviews confirmed the findings in the broader literature that the RMG sector, particularly the knitwear subsector, has enormous backward linkages especially with accessories units. The woven sector has fewer backward linkages for sourcing fabric than the knitwear sector since the majority of manufacturers import their fabrics from countries such as China and India. In the 1990s, value addition in the RMG sector was 20 percent, but this had risen to around 45 percent by 2006. In the knitwear sector, about 85–90 percent of the raw material demand is met by local knitting and knit-dyeing mills, whereas in the woven sector, only about 25 percent of the total woven fabric demand is met by local weaving and processing mills.[47] When asked about their preference for foreign fabrics, some manufacturers claimed that the price of imported fabric was lower than the domestic fabric and a few claimed its quality was superior. Moreover some of them had established relationships with certain Chinese fabric manufacturers. In general, there was a consensus that if the domestic fabric production expanded, they would be more willing to use them since it would reduce lead time considerably.

In addition to obvious linkages, such as with accessories, transportation, banking, and insurance, the interviewees pointed to the less obvious but other equally crucial linkages. They noted that, for example, the huge influx of women in the labor force led to an increased demand for products such as cosmetics and clothing. This, in turn, led to increased spending on advertising of these products, which mainly benefited television channels. All of the interviewees unanimously stated that any setback to the RMG sector would have disastrous consequences for the entire economy because of its linkages with the rest of the economy.

3.4.6. Linkages between RMG Manufacturers

While there were few instances of domestic joint-venture arrangements in the RMG sector, firms generally had close ties with each other. It was easier to verify this for Dhaka and Chittagong, because some interviewees said that at times, if they had a large order, they subcontracted it to RMG manufacturers within their known circle. Some RMG manufacturers also mentioned that they lent their machinery to another firm within their known circle if it needed a piece of equipment for a special order.

3.4.7. Local-Foreign Partnerships

Two of the more notable local-foreign partnerships in the RMG sector were the Desh-Daewoo collaboration in 1979 and the collaboration between Youngones Corporation of South Korea and Trexim Ltd. of Bangladesh in 1980.[48] The latter was the first equity joint venture between a Bangladeshi and a foreign firm. Most of the interviewees replied in the negative when asked about partnerships with foreign firms. The two exceptions were Florence Fabrics Ltd., which entered into a partnership with an Italian firm called Demerc, and BSA Garments, which formed a partnership with one of their fabric suppliers in Singapore, whereby the foreign partner provided 50 percent start-up capital. BSA Garments also sent 30 of their employees to China for technical training. However, in 1984, there were problems regarding the availability of quotas, and the foreign partner retreated. While the majority of the firms interviewed did not have any existing foreign partnership arrangement, they all expressed a desire to form such an arrangement should an opportunity arise.

3.4.8. Compliance Issues

Most of the interviewees replied very confidently in the affirmative when asked whether their factories complied with labor, environmental, and other standards of buyers. They mentioned that U.S. buyers such as Walmart had very strict standards, and they had to conform to the buyers' standards if they wanted to continue doing business with them. Some interviewees noted that European buyers were generally not as strict as the U.S. buyers. Others expressed some frustration that there was no uniform, accepted compliance standard that would be recognized by both European and U.S. buyers. Besides, manufacturers said that sometimes buyers were extremely particular about small details, such as availability of hand washing soap in the restroom.[49]

An RMG manufacturer, who has been in the industry for a long time, said that in the initial stages of the development of the RMG sector, it was easier to set up business. Now, due to stricter compliance rules, the land and premises have to be owned by the company, and the capital investment for a compliant factory is much higher.

3.5. Post-MFA Scenario

There had been many dire predictions regarding the survival of Bangladesh's RMG sector in the post-MFA era. For example, OECD (2004) noted that a global business model based on production fragmentation is economically very vulnerable in the new trade environment without export quotas. Furthermore, in the absence of import quota restrictions in high-income countries, manufacturers in countries that can produce both textiles and clothing are at a competitive advantage. This is because they can avoid the transport costs, time delays, and management time needed to coordinate a production chain where shirts or seat covers, for example, are cut out in one country and stitched together in another. Thus, after the quota phase-out, the most vulnerable were predicted to be the small and remote low-income countries and the lowest-income countries (such as Bangladesh) that were mainly engaged in assembly.

Despite these predictions, the RMG manufacturers in Bangladesh were optimistic about the future of the RMG sector. They observed that while many people had posited China as a threat to the Bangladeshi RMG sector, wages and standards of living in China were rising. This will make it difficult for China to compete in low value-added products with Bangladesh (see Table 3.4).

Given that Bangladesh had a head start, Bangladeshi manufacturers were also not overly concerned about the impact of the United States Trade Development Act of 2000, which allows duty-free and quota-free access to the U.S. market for textiles and apparel exports from sub-Saharan African and the Caribbean Basin Initiative countries. Manufacturers however expressed concerns about competitors such as Vietnam. Most interviewees claimed that with the proper industrial policy support from the government of Bangladesh, the RMG sector could continue to retain its position of strength in the global market for apparels.

This confidence is well placed given that the initial export data show a robust increase in exports post January 1, 2005. The trade data show that RMG imports from Bangladesh to the United States increased by 20 percent in the post-MFA period as compared with the pre-MFA period. The corresponding growth rates for Bangladesh's South Asian competitors, namely, India, Pakistan, and Sri Lanka were 25.7 percent, 13.1 percent, and 5.8 percent respectively (see Tables 3.2 and 2.3).[50] Bangladesh to date has a record in the garment sector to be proud of, considering its initial role in the value chain of a mere assembler and its lack of raw material base. It now has a dynamic and growing textile industry, notwithstanding the constraints faced, and is competing with all comers.

Summary and Conclusion

The success of Bangladesh's RMG sector is all the more remarkable because of its ability to flourish despite domestic constraints such as the lack of a raw material base, political unrest, corruption, and infrastructural constraints. From its modest beginnings as a nontraditional and negligible source of exports, the RMG sector has grown to become Bangladesh's main export revenue earner. The phenomenal growth of the woven RMG sector and specifically of the manufacture of men's shirts can partly be attributed to the crucial Desh-Daewoo partnership that allowed the diffusion of technology and trained personnel. The MFA quotas also helped divert foreign buyers to Bangladesh, since established producers such as Hong Kong and Korea were constrained by quotas. The civil war in Sri Lanka also proved to be of advantage to Bangladesh as many buyers shifted their orders. Domestic government policies such as the introduction of back-to-back L/C, bonded warehouses, cash subsidies to promote backward linkages, and an export-friendly policy environment aided the growth of the sector.

The data demonstrated that Bangladesh has in fact not been a net loser from the quota phaseout in 2005. The RMG sector has continued to enjoy robust growth. However, despite the sustained long-run growth of the RMG sector, there are domestic and foreign constraints that will largely determine its future.

The findings reported in this chapter and our literature review suggest that the value addition in the woven RMG sector is much lower than in the knitwear sector because of the large proportion of imported raw material content in the former. This is one reason why in recent years the growth of the knitwear sector has outpaced that of the woven sector. However, the use of locally produced fabrics reduces lead time and allows RMG manufacturers to avail themselves of preferential market access such as the GSP facilities in the EU market due to rules of origin qualifications. The rapid growth in the knitwear sector can be viewed as a manufacturer response to changing market conditions. Also, a majority of the interviewees have diversified into other products besides basic shirts.

Future growth strategies should focus on the knitwear sector since the value addition is higher and linkages and export opportunities are greater. There is more scope for RMG manufacturers to offer buyers their own fabric, patterns, and designs, and all this leads to further domestic value addition. Thus Bangladesh should transfer the expertise gained in low value-added manufacturing to higher value-added sectors of the supply chain; apparel made from locally produced "ethnic" fabrics is one possibility.

In addition, Bangladesh should more aggressively pursue both duty free access and bilateral and regional cooperation initiatives.[51]

Future administrations need to continue to pursue an active industrial and support policy. To begin with, they would have to address the port bottleneck and the corruption in customs. Venturing into higher value-added products requires investment in the education and training of the labor force. Finally, the government could institute a country-wide uniform compliance standard that is recognized by both European and North American buyers. Different compliance standards for individual buyers are problematic.

It has been noted in this chapter that the garments sector has contributed enormously to the economy in terms of the foreign exchange earnings as well as the employment generation and linkages with other sectors. With appropriate industrial policy and manufacturing strategies, the RMG sector can continue to be a successful driver of export-oriented manufacturing growth. To attain long-term sustainability, Bangladesh will have to diversify in terms of its products as well as markets. The present heavy reliance on the EU and U.S. markets is a limiting strategy since Bangladesh is already facing competition in these markets, but the shift to other markets in 2005–2006 is a good sign.

CHAPTER 4

The Readymade Garment Sector in India

4.1. Introduction

The major markets for Indian RMG products are United States, European Union, Canada, United Arab Emirates, and Australia. With the phaseout of the MFA in 2005, Indian exporters performed better than competitors from most countries to make significant inroads in the U.S. and EU markets. In 2005, RMG exports from India to the United States and to the European Union, two markets that account for over 70 percent of Indian textile and clothing exports, grew at 34.2 percent and 30.6 percent respectively (refer to Table 4.2).[1] India's share of the global apparel market stands at 4 percent,[2] and it is the best performer in South Asia post-MFA (Table 2.3). The market indications and trends are positive and very much in favor of India being recognized as a manufacturing hub for apparels, especially in the higher value-added segment.

The objective of this chapter is to determine the factors accounting for the export success of the Indian RMG sector. It examines a range of strengths, strategies, policies, and partnerships at different stages of the value chain that have built the export competitiveness of this sector. It also examines the threats and weaknesses that undermine its immense potential. Since the sector is predominantly cotton based and, to a large extent, made up of woven apparel, this study focuses more on woven readymade cotton garments.

This chapter is largely based on qualitative inputs and feedback from all the key players and stakeholders in the RMG sector, as described in section 4.3, and supplemented with secondary data.[3] Section 4.2 profiles the post-MFA growth of the sector, following which we turn to a description of the fieldwork. Section 4.4 recounts the factors that account for the success and challenges of the Indian garment industry.

4.2. Post-MFA Growth of the RMG Sector

The export-intensive RMG sector contributes significantly to the Indian economy in terms of output, employment, and foreign exchange earnings. It accounts for 8.37 percent of total exports and 49 percent of textile exports.[4] India currently exports more than 100 product categories, mainly ladies' blouses, men's shirts, T-shirts, and dresses. Cotton apparel exports dominate the RMG sector contributing 80 percent by value.[5] The dismantling of MFA quotas on January 1, 2005, proved to be a watershed for the country's apparel industry. As Table 4.1 indicates, this sector experienced accelerated growth of 31.2 percent in its exports in the year following the phaseout, much higher than previous years.[6]

The high growth of RMG exports is projected to continue and peak at 35.9 percent in 2009–2010 at a value of around $24 billion dollars.[7] Table 4.2 disaggregates the growth rate by major markets.

Table 4.2 shows that even in the second year following the MFA phaseout, the apparel export growth was in double digits in both markets.

Table 4.1 Export growth, value, and export share of the RMG sector in India

Period	Percentage growth	Fiscal year	Value (mil. $s)	RMG as a % of total exports
2004–2005 to 2005–2006	31.22	2005–2006	8,626.63	8.37
2003–2004 to 2004–2005	5.30	2004–2005	6,573.97	7.85
2002–2003 to 2003–2004	8.79	2003–2004	6,243.12	9.78
2001–2002 to 2002–2003	14.60	2002–2003	5,738.44	10.88
2000–2001 to 2001–2002	NA	2001–2002	5,007.53	11.43

NA: not available.
Source: Government of India, Directorate General of Central Intelligence Statistics (2006).

Table 4.2 Percentage growth in Indian apparel and textile exports to the top two quota markets

Commodity	2005	Jan–May 2006
United States		
Apparel	34.2	19.54
Textiles	16.43	13.29
European Union		
	2005	Jan–March 2006
Apparel	30.6	25.8
Textiles	2.2	2.4

Source: Ministry of Textiles, Government of India (2006).

Table 4.3 Growth trends of knitted vs. woven apparel and total RMG exports of India

Commodity	2002–2003		2003–2004		2004–2005		2005–2006		Share of total exports (2005–2006) (%)
	Value	Growth	Value	Growth	Value	Growth	Value	Growth	
Apparel and clothing accessories, knitted or crocheted	2,386.7	28.04	2,701.8	13.2	2,641.3	−2.2	3,191.1	20.8	3.1
Apparel and clothing accessories, not knitted or crocheted	3,351.8	6.6	3,541.4	5.7	3,932.7	11.1	5,435.5	38.2	5.3
India's total RMG exports	5,738.4	14.6	6,243.1	8.8	6,574.0	5.3	8,626.6	31.2	8.4
India's total exports	52,719.4	20.3	63,842.9	21.1	83,535.9	30.9	103,090.5	23.4	

Source: UN TRAINS (2007), www.untrains.com.

While RMG firms are spread all over the country, the main clusters are currently located in the National Capital Region (NCR), Mumbai, Bengaluru, Tirupur/Coimbatore, and Ludhiana, and they collectively employ about 3.5 million people[8] out of the 35 million people directly employed by the textile and clothing sector.[9] It is estimated that there are 65,000 garment units in the organized sector in India, of which about 88 percent make woven garments, while the remaining make knitwear.[10] Table 4.3 outlines the leading position held by woven garments in the Indian RMG sector and shows that woven apparel alone accounts for 5.3 percent of the country's total exports, whereas knitted and crocheted apparel account for 3.1 percent.

As Table 4.3 shows, woven garments also experienced much higher post-MFA growth at 38.2 percent in 2005–2006.

4.3. Fieldwork

Prior to the field interviews in India, desk research identified two major products from among India's RMG exports that had indicated high-value growth over a decade (refer to Table 1.2). These leading products are ladies' woven cotton blouses and men's woven cotton shirts, which in 2005–2006

Table 4.4 Indian export trends of selected products and overall for the RMG sector

Years	Value of total exports	Value of RMG exports	Value of men's shirts	Value of ladies' blouses
2001–2002	43,826.7	5,007.5	569.8	505.2
2002–2003	52,719.0	5,738.4	604.0	701.0
2003–2004	63,843.0	6,243.1	609.3	625.3
2004–2005	83,535.9	6,574.0	625.1	734.9
2005–2006	103,090.5	8,626.6	688.1	1,018.0

Source: UN TRAINS (2007), www.untrains.com.

had export values of $1.018 billion and $688 million, respectively, out of the total RMG exports of $8.6 billion.[11] Thus these products together accounted for one-fifth of the RMG exports and also demonstrated steady high growth, as shown in Table 4.4.

The basis for identifying interviewees among successful RMG manufacturers and buyers was the performance of their products in the export market. With these field interviews, we were able to assess the supply-side factors accounting for the export competitiveness of the RMG sector in general and of these products in particular.

Field interviews were conducted in the major export hubs of Delhi/NCR, Mumbai, Bengaluru/Yeshwantpur, and Tirupur/Palladam, with RMG entrepreneurs, company executives, government officials, agents of garment buying houses, and leaders of producer/exporter associations. Interviews could only be arranged on the basis of contacts, and therefore a random sample was not possible. However, a range of firms were covered—from the biggest exporting houses to small- and medium-sized firms in different regions of India. This selection helped us gain a diversity of perspectives.[12]

Although there was one standard format for questions (Annexures 1.1 and 1.2), many interviews were tailored for the individual interviewees. While some interviewees were responsive and gave in-depth answers and information, many did not go into details. Almost all were reluctant to share financial information and the contact information of their foreign partners or buyers. As is generally true in this volume, there was a glaring gap between the government official's and the firm manager's versions regarding the government's contribution and support to the sector.[13]

4.4. Findings

This section explores the strengths, strategies, partnerships, and policy environment that have led to the export success of the RMG sector. Using ladies' woven cotton blouses and men's shirts as leading products in the apparel sector, this section outlines certain specialties and lacunae present at different stages of the value chain in the textile and clothing industry. While these findings are based largely on interviews with entrepreneurs, RMG company executives, and government officials, they have been supplemented with secondary data as earlier stated.

4.4.1. Factors Accounting for Success

India has a competitive raw material advantage in cotton garments, as it has a strong cotton production base. It is the third-largest producer of cotton and the second-largest producer of cotton yarn in the world. Cotton production increased significantly in India from 15.8 million bales in 2002 to 24.4 million bales in 2006,[14] ensuring the availability of raw cotton to the domestic textile industry at competitive prices. The production of cotton fiber therefore increased at an impressive annual growth rate of 11.48 percent between 2002–2003 and 2005–2006.[15]

Along with the raw material advantage, the labor-intensive RMG sector also benefits from low labor costs. India compares very favorably in terms of labor cost per hour with developed countries like the United States, the countries of European Union, and competitors like China, Taiwan, and Korea. Only countries such as Bangladesh, Pakistan and Vietnam have labor costs marginally lower than India. The wage rate for the Indian textile sector is around US$0.75 per operator hour, compared with US$1 for China and US$3 for Turkey.[16] Though the productivity of Indian workers is lower due to low level of technology and poor organization,[17] India still has an advantage over China in labor costs, after accounting for labor productivity, that is, it has lower unit labor costs.[18] Moreover, India is rich in traditional workers adept at adding value with tasks such as embroidery, mirror work, beading, and making complex garments.[19] Both these factors provide the textile and clothing sector with a competitive edge in the global market.

The clothing industry is fragmented and predominantly small-scale. There are 12,963 units (excluding tailoring units)—of which 12,289 are small-scale industry (SSI) units and 674 non-SSI units.[20] Major manufacturers each have at least 18–20 units set up separately, whereas an equivalent Indonesian or Chinese company would have only two or three units.[21] This fragmentation can be attributed partly to the tax exemptions provided to SSI units and to the reservation of woven apparels and knitwear for the SSI sector until 2001 and 2005 respectively.[22]

The quota policy that prevailed under the MFA quota regime until 2005 also did not encourage the consolidation of units. However, subsequent to the MFA phaseout and dereservation during the Tenth Five Year Plan period

(2002–2007), the process of consolidation and mergers in the clothing sector has started and companies are expanding. Different establishments, especially in South India, have started organizing into clusters or into bigger, integrated units with all processes under one roof: dyeing, weaving, washing, cutting, and stitching. Several clothing units have also taken advantage of the government's Technological Upgradation Fund Scheme (TUFS) to expand and modernize their units. Nevertheless, the consolidation process has been slow due to prevailing labor laws and the high cost of land,[23] which facilitates the trend toward the establishment of small units.[24]

This fragmentation implies that the Indian apparel industry has not been able to benefit from the economies of scale of specialized assembly lines prevalent in garment factories in China, Vietnam, Cambodia, and Thailand. Fragmentation hinders productivity and investment, and limits rationalization of the workforce. While fragmentation is a weakness in many ways, India has used it to its advantage. India's cultivation of a niche in low-volume, detailed, and stylized garments is diametrically opposite to China's specialization in basic garments produced on a large scale. India's operational flexibility and ability to handle smaller volumes with multiple levels of value addition have now becomes its unique selling point. A diverse design base, traditional designs, and embellishments, such as sequins, prints, handiwork, embroidery, mirror and glasswork, make Indian garments uncommon. The RMG sector has succeeded in combining the diverse strengths of the domestic handloom and other traditional skills with new international developments to produce a range of distinctive garments. India thus specializes in product differentiation in mid- to high-end fashion garments to answer the requirements of small orders ranging from 500 to 10,000 pieces.[25]

There is also a geographical specialization in production. Ladies' blouses, which have more detailed designs and trimmings, are usually produced in North India, which is known for its traditional strengths in designs and embellishments. Men's dress shirts and printed casual wear shirts, competitive items of Indian companies made on a large scale, are produced mainly in South India, which has larger and more organized factories.

Most firms interviewed attributed their strength to their flexibility that allowed for product diversification and to their ability to produce a variety of goods that ensured a wider range of buyers. Companies are thus able to produce garments for men, women, and children, and to cater to both high-end and low-end buyers and small and big volumes. A medium-sized company like Sonal Garments can make high-end $7–$15 ladies' blouses with embellishments for Victoria's Secret, but also cheap $1.5 shirts for children's clothing and maternity wear.[26]

Some large companies, such as Alok Industries, offer a versatile product range of apparel fabrics, home textiles, and readymade garments, thus providing complete sourcing solutions for many of the world's leading brands and retailers. Alok Industries spans across the value chain and its activities include spinning, texturizing, weaving, knitting, yarn and fabric processing, embroidery, and garment production and testing. The vertically integrated operations and flexibility enable the company to meet all its client requirements and thus provide integrated textile solutions. Such firms have benefited from branching out from the initial one or two categories to eight to ten categories. Their lack of specialization and assortment of products have not proved to be their weakness.[27]

However, some leading companies find it better to specialize than to be a Jack-of-all-trades.[28] For example, Madura Garments specializes in formal wear for men[29] and Royal Embroidery specializes in children's wear.[30] Specialization allows for economies of scale, better quality, faster delivery, and improved efficiencies. Product specialization allows some factories to improve efficiencies to levels even better than those of many Chinese firms. For example, Gokaldas Images has 18 specialized garment manufacturing facilities with stringent sampling and quality control systems. It has expansive in-house facilities, which include an in-house textile quality lab, washing facilities, multihead embroidery, and a single Web-based information system connecting all operations.[31]

Large players with global ambitions, such as Gokaldas Exports and Madura Garments, keep abreast of fashions by visiting fairs, shows, and exhibitions. By visiting exhibitions abroad, such as in Milan and Paris, company executives get design ideas to incorporate into their products. They also themselves put up exhibitions every three or four months, for each season, for buyers to select designs.[32] Creativity, design, innovation, and product development make these firms stand apart. Market leaders like Gokaldas Images and Madura Garments have both achieved many "firsts" and spearheaded development of certain product categories. For example, Madura Garments pioneered wrinkle-free shirts and trousers in India[33] (explained later), while Gokaldas Images was one of the first to produce suits, intimate wear, and outerwear on a large scale.[34]

Hemchandra Javeri, President, Madura Garments, stated, "We are not in the business of exports. We are in the business of creating identities." Brand promotion, in today's consumer-oriented market, is vital for Indian firms to penetrate markets and realize higher unit values. Brands give an assurance of quality, durability, and conformity to social, environmental, and quality standards.

North American and European markets that account for more than 70 percent of Indian apparel exports are dominated by various global brands, and Indian exporters are the main suppliers to these brands.[35] It is estimated that the final retail value of an apparel product sold to consumers in export markets is 5 to 10 times higher than its factory price.[36] As a result, many Indian exporters are losing out on a significant amount of export earnings due to poor brand development. Brand development can help Indian firms move up the value chain, increase the market share and acceptability of Indian apparel, and record higher export earnings.[37]

One of the key differentiating factors for market leaders like Madura Garments and Gokaldas Images is thus their focus on branding by creating fashions and building identities. Madura Garments launched brand names like Allen Solly and Peter England in men's formal wear, whereas Gokaldas Images introduced brands like Weekender and Weekender Kids that focused on youth fashion and children's wear, respectively. These are leading brands in their segments in terms of size, brand appeal, and market influence. Such firms are therefore not cut-and-make operators or converters. To increase their share of the pie, they have invested not only in manufacturing and exporting products, but also in image creation.[38] Indian companies are also acquiring foreign companies and brands that enjoy considerable popularity in their home markets. For example, Welspun has acquired UK-based Christy, Malwa Industries has acquired Italy-based Emmetre, and Alok Industries has bought UK-based Hamsard.

The success of the Indian garment industry can also be attributed to Indian entrepreneurship. For example, while Bangladesh and Sri Lanka have demonstrated success (see chapters 3 and 7), there is still a great deal of dependency for designs and style for textiles and garments. Indian business leaders have done much groundwork in this regard. They have toured buyer countries, examined their markets firsthand, and developed products suited to those markets. Indian exporters have had a long learning curve in dealing with foreign buyers and have gained ample experience in the field of international business. Entrepreneurs claim that Indian companies have created the business instead of having it handed to them.[39] In China, it has been large public entities and corporations, the government, and Hong Kong-based entrepreneurs who have invested in the Chinese economy. By contrast, they claim that in India, it is the local entrepreneurs who have done the legwork and developed the industry from a low initial level to where it is today. In the process, small family companies have grown into relatively large businesses.

Indian companies like Madura Garments also often employ "geographic" strategies. Certain countries have little or no tariff barriers with the

United States; so production is set up in those countries (refer also to chapter 5 on Nepal in this volume). For example, viscose garments are produced in Egypt as they face no tariff in the United States, as opposed to a 30 percent tariff that applies to the export from China. This 30 percent benefit is shared with customers.[40] Companies like Madura Garments therefore consider themselves as a 'one stop solution provider.'[41]

4.4.2. Challenges

Bellyaching by business leaders, company managers, and members of industrial associations is a constant refrain throughout the book and seems more so the case in India. It appears as if they often complain without a reason. Given the spectacular success of Indian industry, clearly, not all is going wrong. Nonetheless, the continuing constraints alluded to in this section need policy attention to enhance and sustain success.

The nonavailability of quality workforce is a dampener to growth in this sector. Out of 5.57 million workers in the garment sector, it is estimated that 2.5 million are employed in the export sector.[42] The maximum incremental requirement for workers is in the RMG sector, and this demand is projected to almost double to 11.22 million workers in the next five years.[43]

The apparel industry is also facing a shortage of more than 500,000 trained workers.[44] It is estimated that training facilities need to be increased three- to fourfold to meet the demand for trained labor. According to the Working Group on Textiles and Jute Industry of the Ministry of Textiles (2006), 450,000 operators, 22,000 jobbers, 11,000 pattern makers, 11,000 technicians/quality controllers and 6,000 managers are required. The working group has also estimated the incremental manpower requirement at 17.37 million, with 12.02 million workers needed directly in the apparel industry and 5.35 million workers in the ancillary industry.

Labor shortage makes it hard for small companies to find and retain skilled workers as they always leave if they are offered higher wages elsewhere.[45] Firms like Sonal Garments are tackling the short supply of skilled labor by training workers in dedicated factories of about 100 machines. Sonal garments recruits people, trains them rigorously for six months, and then assigns them to company factories.[46] Firms also help improve labor productivity by providing provident funds, social security benefits, healthy and hygienic conditions, and facilities such as cafeterias and crèches (which are important as 38 percent of workers are women).[47]

The RMG sector also faces structural and technological weaknesses in weaving, processing, and garmenting due to low investments. Indian firms have an average of 119 machines compared with 605 in China.[48] The low level of investment in the Indian apparel sector has led to nonavailability of indigenous textile machinery for knitting and garmenting. As much as 50 to 60 percent of the machinery for the clothing industry needs to be imported, and the excise duty makes it more expensive.[49] Therefore, many processes, equipment, and machines are outdated. Indian firms have a much higher proportion of manual machines.[50] For example, the shuttleless looms in India are only 2 percent of the total looms, which is much below the world average of 16 percent. Competitors like China and Pakistan have a higher proportion of shuttleless looms at 15 and 9 percent, respectively.[51] Reputed textile machinery manufacturers have set up units in China and have developed models suitable to the Chinese industry.[52] The domestic availability of textile machinery in China has helped trigger the growth of the country's RMG sector and given it an advantage over the Indian RMG sector (refer to Table 2.3).

The Indian industry also faces other disadvantages: the interest rates on term loans for the textile and clothing industry are high in India. At 11 percent per annum, at the time of writing (mid-2008), it was much higher than that in other competing countries, for example, 2.5 percent and 3.5 percent, respectively, in Taiwan and Malaysia.[53]

Indian garment exporters also face high transaction costs, which, however, have fallen from 15 percent of the export revenues, in 1998, to 3–10 percent in 2006.[54] In part, the high transaction cost results from various taxes on interstate movement of goods due to absence of a uniform duty structure across states,[55] corruption by government officials, and delays in obtaining customs clearances or refunds from duty drawbacks.[56]

Transportation within India is ridden with delays. For example, goods from Chennai take 12 days to reach Bengaluru, the same amount of time that it takes goods to reach Chennai from China.[57] From a Creative Enterprises factory in Daman, 180 kilometers from the port in Mumbai, transportation time would only be four hours in high-income countries, but the factory sends goods a day ahead of time to avoid possible delays.[58] Businesses also face many delays due to documentation and customs, even while importing material. Entrepreneurs therefore universally emphasized the need to build infrastructure and streamline processes to avoid delays and reduce costs. Cluster development has helped cut down on transaction time and costs to a certain extent, as products are no longer required to be sent to different cities for different value-added processes (refer to subsection 4.4.4.2).

There are inordinate delays due to infrastructural problems in roads, railways, and seaports. A mother vessel cannot berth in India, unlike in

Colombo, Singapore, or Dubai, due to the limited capacity of the ports.[59] This implies longer delivery times and higher freight costs. For example, it is more expensive to ship a consignment to the United States from Mumbai than from Bangladesh or even China, as a feeder ship from Mumbai has to take the consignment to Colombo or Singapore and then transfer it to a mother vessel for the United States.[60] India's geographical distance from European and U.S. markets also makes it hard to compete on delivery times, since, on average, shipping time from India to the United States is 28 days compared with two days from Mexico.[61] A 20-day ocean voyage is said to be the equivalent of a 16 percent import tariff.[62]

The availability, quality, and cost of electricity also add to the problems of the Indian RMG sector. The cost of power is much higher in India at nine cents per kilowatt-hour than in Pakistan, Bangladesh, and China at five cents.[63] Moreover, due to acute power shortage, entrepreneurs, for example in the NCR, have to resort to captive generation, which doubles the cost.[64] Power cost that amounts to 8 percent of the sale value weakens India's export competitiveness.[65] High power costs also discourage potential Foreign Direct Investment (FDI), partnerships that could be a source of technology acquisition and marketing information.

India's stringent labor laws (refer to subsection 4.4.4.2) constrain hiring and firing and contract labor, and therefore are unfavorable to the largely seasonal garment industry with short fashion cycles and lead times. These rigid labor laws have also restricted the flow of investment and entry of firms into the apparel industry. It is estimated that three million new jobs would be created in garment manufacturing alone under a more flexible labor law regime.[66]

This industry is also hamstrung by a range of other regulations and taxes. For example, environmental regulations often serve the Pollution Control Board as a pretext for delays and bribes. An industry representative reported, "There are 36 inspectors who have absolute authority to close my factory. They could close down my firm even if it has two bulbs more than the number consistent with the factory capacity."

Our interviewees pointed out that in the United States, a firm is able to file bankruptcy so that another company can take it over and infuse capital and restructure it for higher efficiency. The Indian exit policy under the Industrial Dispute Act (1947) requires prior state government approval to close factories, which is hard to get and involves bribes. One entrepreneur phrased the situation as "*Na jeenay detay hain, na marnay detay hain*" ("They don't let us live, nor do they let us die"). The RMG sector faces 54 kinds of taxes and duties, including octroi duties, electricity duty, fringe benefits taxes, entry tax, and sales tax, which have still not been simplified or made uniform.[67]

Apart from supply-side constraints, there are also external conditions that can impede the spectacular growth of Indian RMG exports. The elimination of quotas has led to increased market competition and price pressures. During the quota regime, the competition was limited to the firms with quota allocations. The dismantling of quotas has been followed by the entry of new small and medium manufacturers, not only within India but also from other countries where firms confronted similar quotas prior to the MFA phaseout.[68] RMG exporters who were at an advantage when they had quotas are now experiencing shrinking profit margins and are turning toward the domestic market, where they feel there is a growing opportunity for scale increases and profits.[69] Many RMG manufacturers are considering supplying goods to companies like Reliance for retail sale in the domestic market, which they would never have considered in the past.[70]

Exchange rate trends also play an important role in garment exports. The garment sector managed to do well in the 1990s due to the decline of the Indian rupee against the U.S. dollar. As pointed out by Hashim (2005), this brought down the unit cost of production at constant prices in dollars terms, even though the real cost increased due to poor productivity. According to the Government of India (2006a), the revaluation of the Chinese yuan by around 2.05 percent also helped India to some extent in becoming price competitive vis-à-vis China in items such as women's blouses and men's shirts. In contrast, the appreciation of the Indian rupee (2006–2008) has hurt apparel exporters. The Indian rupee appreciated by 11.2 percent from Rs. 44.4 to Rs. 39.4 to a dollar in this period.[71] Since buyers compare the prices of products from different countries on the basis of the U.S. dollar, the continuing appreciation of the Indian rupee against the dollar could weaken India's competitive position and profits.[72]

4.4.3. The Role of Partnerships

There are many forms of partnership and linkages in the RMG sector for technological support, product development, design work, marketing activities, and supply chain alignment.

4.4.3.1. Horizontal Partnerships

There is little active horizontal integration and cooperation between RMG manufacturers. As the Indian apparel industry in most areas is fragmented and competitive, most companies find that there is limited scope for partnerships with other RMG firms. There is a degree of cooperation when complementarities exist between firms. For example, in case of orders that exceed capacity, it is common for firms to utilize each other's production capacity and embroidery facilities, especially within a cluster. While it is common for exporters to discuss problems and difficulties in their exporters' associations, there is usually little exchange of information and active cooperation. There are, however, some exceptions.

Family ties can play an important role in fostering business cooperation in the RMG sector. K. Mohan, along with its subsidiaries, is owned by brothers. They cooperate by mutually sharing information and links and recommending buyers and suppliers to each other.[73]

The members of Okhla Garments and Textiles Cluster (OGTC) have organized joint training for their workers and have hired professional lobbyists to interface with the government.[74] Through data sharing on costs and best practices and common sourcing, members are able to reduce costs effectively. For example, OGTC members collectively purchased 1.6 million meters of viscose georgette and benefited from a collective saving of Rs. 3.2 million.[75] The most well-known exception, however, is the Tirupur Exporters' Association (TEA), whose collaborative achievements include multibillion-dollar projects. The Tirupur Exporters' Association has been adopted as a UNIDO (United Nations Industrial Development Organization) model, and their accomplishments are described below.[76]

4.4.3.2. Cluster Development

Clusters are an important development in the RMG sector that help in overcoming supply-chain difficulties including short delivery periods and tight logistics.[77] Clusters are able to build synergies and negotiate for services, as is most apparent in the case of the Tirupur cluster. For example, whereas one power-loom unit can only make a limited range of products on its own, it is possible to make a wide range of items in an apparel park. Individual power-loom units that lack assets and markets are able to become bankable, attain creditworthiness, and benefit from economies of scale when they come together as consortiums in apparel parks.[78] Apparel parks and clusters have thus helped overcome structural deficiencies of smaller individual manufacturing units. Textile clusters have developed in and around Ludhiana, Bengaluru, Mumbai, Delhi, Indore, Jaipur, and Tirupur.

Tirupur is the largest garment cluster in India. In 2006, it was responsible for US$1.5 billion of exports, and its total value of production was US$2.5 billion (including both the export and the domestic markets).[79] Tirupur also boasts of exemplary partnerships and cooperation between firms and has taken huge strides by establishing textile and apparel parks.

Tirupur is largely driven by the ethnic community of Goundars, with leaders like Sakthivel. There is a lot of collaborative behavior in Tirupur that manifests itself in the TEA headed by Sakthivel. Tirupur's model is based on "collaborating while competing."[80] Firms compete in the market while collaborating in business operations.

Tirupur has faced adverse conditions, but the unique collaboration with TEA has helped in overcoming them. For example, Tirupur is rain deficient, and in response, Rs. 3.5 billion worth of water supplies were brought in every year in tankers from a distance of 30–40 kilometers.[81] Infrastructure Leasing & Financial Services Ltd. (IL&FS) was building a Rs. 10 billion project in collaboration with local exporters to pump water from the Kaveri river.[82]

The TEA has cooperated on a range of other projects—common effluent treatment plants, industrial parks, an exhibition center, integrated textile parks, and a fashion institute. For each project, the TEA formed a new company as a joint venture between TEA, IL&FS, and the Government of Tamil Nadu. Such special purpose venture companies (SPVs) are established through government grants, bank loans, and TEA's own contribution for each initiative. The TEA has engaged in a diverse range of activities. For example, it set up a public school for children, the Sardar Vallabhbhai Patel Institute of Textile Management, and a fashion institute, initially in collaboration with National Institute of Fashion Technology (NIFT). It coordinates exhibitions and negotiates with the labor unions and fixes wages every two years.[83]

For all major projects, TEA procured funding, all at the initiative of the user industry. TEA is also responsible for the only functional integrated textile park in India—Netaji Apparel Park—for which it made use of the government's Scheme for Integrated Textile Parks (SITP) with a project cost of Rs. 1.3 billion. Under the user-driven SITP scheme, TEA set up both the Netaji Apparel Park and the Palladam Hi-Tech Weaving Park with a 20 percent contribution from the users, 40 percent from the government (Rs. 400 million), and a 40 percent bank loan through IL&FS assistance.[84]

An SPV was initiated for this Hi-Tech Weaving Park in which all users had equity depending on their contribution. The bank lent 40 percent of the project cost to the SPV, which is to be paid back in 12 years by the users. A Debt Service Fund is maintained through contributions from all participating firms, in case any borrower defaults.[85]

The Netaji Park is a Rs. 1 billion project that became functional on January 10, 2005. There are now 60 units with an investment of Rs. 20 million per unit. Firms benefit from reduced costs and improved logistics by operating in proximity to each other. In this massive complex, along with the units for textile firms, there is a common facility center, banks, and stores for needles and accessories. There is a branch of the State Bank of India, which has 3,000–4,000 worker accounts and nine company salary accounts. There are also plans to establish hostels for the workers, but meanwhile, firms such as the Texport Syndicate provide transportation for their workers.[86]

Near Tirupur, the 65-acre Palladam Hi-Tech Weaving Park was under construction during our fieldwork (it is now operational). There were 78 units of 6 shuttleless looms, 4 units of 24 looms, 12 units of 12 looms, 1 unit of 18 looms, and 1 sizing unit for raw material. They also had a crèche, a testing lab, a training center, a health center, an ATM, a bank, a post office, and toilets. The sheds had humidification systems to maintain yarn quality.

The exporters at Tirupur have also made effective use of government's TUFS that provides a 5 percent interest reimbursement on loans for investment in benchmarked technology and machinery. Between 1999 and August 2006, projects worth Rs. 446.9 billion were sanctioned under this scheme.[87] However, the scheme stipulated that the unit size could not exceed the cap of Rs. 10 million to be eligible for subsidy. While the cap is not too high, many exporters in Tirupur have used this scheme to obtain high-tech equipment for knitting, cutting, marking, sewing, ironing, and packing. Industries at Tirupur have taken more advantage of the TUFS scheme than industries elsewhere; the overall usage of this scheme in general has been low.[88]

4.4.3.3. Vertical Integration and Supply-Chain Partnerships

As in the case of horizontal collaboration, family ties can also facilitate vertical collaboration. For example, Indus Fila, a garment manufacturing company, can count on price concessions and an assured supply of fabric from a fabric manufacturing company owned by the same family.[89] However, much of the collaboration naturally happens outside family networks.

While some large firms, such as Alok Industries and Gokaldas Images, have presence throughout the value chain, most RMG firms only manufacture and design garments, and do not make fabric and textiles. Since the major part—40–60 percent[90]—of the production is raw material, good partnerships with vendors can reduce prices and delivery time. It is important to have backward integration and strong business links with companies for sources of raw materials, fabric, buttons, lace, dye, and embroidery to ensure a smooth supply chain and a complete solution for customers. The alignment of firms at different tiers of the supply chain also helps cut down on each firm's marketing costs, which are borne at the final stage of the supply chain.

RMG firms can also partner with first-tier and second-tier mills.[91] This partnership includes strategic cooperation with mills to help capture markets. For example, Vardhaman Mills conceded two to three price drops for Madura Garments to help it compete with Chinese suppliers in securing business orders for a low–cost, low-end product.[92] Due to the price cuts, Madura Garments succeeded in retaining the business, and the profits were shared with the vendor. Cooperation may also be in the form of technology transfer to help mills come up to speed to service RMG firms. Madura Garments has helped Precot Mills in Coimbatore to upgrade its capabilities in technology and processes.[93]

Many companies have also changed their marketing strategy to adapt to the increasingly competitive and constantly changing business environment and the everchanging needs of the customer. For example, Madura Garments markets its products together with Pacific Wave in the United States, so its front-end office in New York attracts U.S. customers and businesses, such as Haggar's (men's wear). For the last 15 years, Madura Garments has had German agents represent it in dealings with German businesses, such as Marco Polo, and Australian agents in Australia to negotiate with brands, such as Quiksilver. The logic for using local agents is: "*A German in Germany is better than an Indian in Germany.*"[94] Gokaldas Images has also set up an office and a showroom in New York to be closer to the clients to meet their requirements. This has helped the company attract and build several international tie-ups and collaborations with brands such as FILA, Nike, Reebok, DKNY, Levis, Tommy, Abercrombie & Fitch, Guess, Ann Taylor, and Liz Claiborne.[95]

Foreign firms can help with technological support, product upgrading, design, and processes to enhance efficiencies. Design, technical know-how, and processes, rather than marketing assistance, are areas where foreign firms in particular collaborate with Indian firms. Foreign buyers have introduced quality concepts and provided capacity building and technological assistance in some cases to Indian firms. When Gokaldas Images started its new product category of suits, Telwood Company based in New York sent technicians to help set up processes.[96] Companies imbibe and make use of customers' quality systems to enhance the confidence placed in them and to foster long-term relationships.

Buyers can also initiate coordination between firms. For example, Indo Polycoats' buyers often place orders with two different firms. However, since the buyer has the same color and quality standards, they require the two firms to coordinate the dying and coloring. In this way, companies are able to learn about other firms' technical processes, machinery, suppliers, and sources.[97]

Foreign buyers have also sought intermediaries in India in the form of buying agencies. As fashions change quickly, the delivery time keeps getting reduced—from 90–100 days a decade ago it dropped to around 60 days in 2007.[98] There is increased competitive pressure on factories, so buyers help firms stick to timelines by delegating approvals to the buying agency they enlist in the country. Buying agencies are able to monitor the firms and can give them feedback on production and help them develop new products. Buying agencies also employ in-house designers and international designers to innovate: for example, Cascade Enterprises, a buying agency in India, has developed a line of batik designs. Foreign buyers rarely get everything from one exporter—they need a range of products from different exporters. The role of buying agencies is to identify the best producer in the market for a particular product. Foreign firms prefer to diversify, so they maintain direct linkages with RMG firms and also seek indirect linkages through buying agencies.[99]

An independent and third-party accreditation or certification of products, processes, and systems has also emerged as a key requirement for the global competitiveness of the Indian textile and clothing industry. Exporting firms are required to conform to quality, environmental, and social standards of foreign firms. There are a set of codes such as nonuse of child labor; provision of crèches, fire exits, and toilets, employee benefits like provident funds; and transparency. Foreign firms like Gap, Walmart, and J. C. Penney employ auditing firms whereas other firms send their own teams to review factories regularly. There are also third-party agencies, such as Societe Generale de Surveillance (SGS), Det Norske Veritas (DNV), and Technischer Überwachungs-Verein (TUV), who carry out audits and certification.

To maintain long-term relationships with customers, it is essential for firms to honor their commitments. For example, during the quota regime, the price of the quota share would at times rise between the time of order and the time of delivery, entailing significant losses for exporting companies. In one such case, Sonal Garments, a medium-sized firm, expected a loss of $2 per garment—but the firm honored its commitment. The firm's reputation for reliability makes buyers go back to it. Buyers are ready to offer a premium, up to ten or twenty cents per item, for reliability.[100]

Buyers are also willing to cooperate and extend concessions to reliable partners. Sometimes, at the sampling stage, the merchandiser prepares a sample without scrutinizing production aspects carefully. It might be a side seam prepared from a double-needle stitch that could be done in a more production-friendly way. Buyers accept feedback from the firm and are willing to concede minor nonstructural changes to make the item more production friendly while maintaining quality and style.[101]

Buyers can also help in other ways. For example, during the MFA quota period, H&M booked a huge order of 200,000 pieces from Sonal Garments, but the quota premiums increased significantly, implying a massive loss for the firm. Given the circumstances, H&M cooperated with Sonal Garments and had the fabric and production shifted to Bangladesh. H&M helped with deliveries and shipments and helped Sonal Garments meet its commitment. H&M need not have permitted the shifting, but then Sonal Garments would have incurred a loss.[102]

While Indian firms enjoy strong and steady relationships with foreign firms, there are still only a limited number of joint ventures in the apparel industry compared with competitors, such as China, and FDI is similarly limited. This is mainly due to regulatory barriers and stringent labor laws in India (refer to subsection 4.4.4.2). In 2005, the total FDI in the clothing and textile sector in India was only 1.8 percent of the total or US $78.99 million, whereas in China the figure was 8.3 per cent or US $5.4 billion.[103] Large-scale apparel units have been set up through foreign investment in China. While foreign firms are setting up mills and fabric-manufacturing facilities in India, there is little foreign investment in garment manufacturing.[104] Silvia Apparels, a joint venture of Mafatlal Apparel and Le Perla, an Italian company, and the Marzotto Group in Delhi are some exceptions, but these are few and far between.[105] Even so, India is ranked as the second-most attractive destination for FDI in the context of foreign investors looking for alternative manufacturing bases to China, and this opportunity needs to be explored.[106]

4.4.3.4. Interindustry Partnerships

There are also partnerships with firms outside the RMG sector for technological upgrading and product development. Firms across industries can work jointly on marketable new products. For example, Madura Garments conducted joint research work with nanotechnology firms for vapor phase technology and with chemical companies, such as Ciba and Clariant, which did the lab testing to develop chemicals with new effects. Such partnerships helped Madura Garments offer pathbreaking products, such as wrinkle-free cotton trousers, to well-known companies, such as Haggar's. Madura Garment's wrinkle-free trousers are now one of the best in the world and they command a premium.[107]

4.4.4. Role of the Government

Government policy has played an important role in influencing the structure and growth of the Indian textile industry. Since the mid-1980s, the government has tried to provide the industry a "friendly" policy environment and initiated schemes to facilitate the growth of the RMG sector. This is partly evident from the industrial policy collaboration in the Tirupur cluster, outlined in subsection 4.4.3.2. However, while the government has made a huge effort to invest in and subsidize the RMG sector, its policies are largely targeted toward small and medium-scale enterprises (SMEs). Most entrepreneurs interviewed therefore did not attribute their success to the government. However, the government recognizes the potential of this sector and is working toward creating a more conducive policy environment for its growth.

With the National Textile Policy of 1985, economic liberalization reforms of 1991, and the National Textile Policy of 2000, the government has taken steps to liberalize regulations and simplify procedures to improve the competitiveness of the textile industry. The rationalization of fiscal duties has provided a level playing field to all segments, resulting in more holistic growth of the industry.[108] The dereservation of woven apparels from the ambit of the SSI sector under the National Textile Policy 2000 has boosted production. Many import restraints and tariffs have been lifted to make way for duty-free imports. For example, under the new Foreign Trade Policy 2004, trimmings and embellishments that are important for value addition in the RMG sector were made exempt from import duty.[109] Duty-free import of trimmings and embellishments for handlooms and handicrafts sectors was increased from 3 percent to 5 percent of free on board (FOB)[110] value of exports.[111] Speed-breakers such as documents and customs have also been reduced.[112] As ports have been privatized, the clearance time for consignments has also reduced from five days to two days.[113]

4.4.4.1. Government Schemes and Support

The government launched TUFS in 1999 to promote modernization in the industry (see subsection 4.4.3.2). The scheme was set up to help the industry to meet its capital needs at internationally comparable rates of interest and to upgrade its technology. It provides 5 percent interest reimbursement for long- and medium-term loans to eligible manufacturing units in the industry. While the response to TUFS was initially slow, it registered a growth of 123 percent and 127 percent over 2005 and 2006, respectively.[114] By August 2006, projects worth Rs. 446.9 billion were sanctioned under TUFS.[115] Nevertheless, the overall response has been low, and entrepreneurs claim that there are not enough incentives for technological upgrading even in TUFS.

To move from shuttle looms to shuttleless looms, three semi-automatic components are required. If only two components are used, the upgrading is not sanctioned under TUFS.[116] There is also a restriction of Rs. 10 million per unit to qualify either for a 5 percent interest subsidy or for a 20 percent cash subsidy. There has been a growing demand from users to increase this cap to Rs. 20 million, and although an order was issued by Ministry of

Textiles in 2006 to this effect, it is yet to be processed and formally issued. Although the subsidy is 20 percent on machinery, the duty is 10 percent, so the net benefit to the industry is just 10 percent. TUFS was set to expire in 2007 with the end of the Tenth Five Year Plan (2002–2007), but the industry has succeeded in obtaining an extension for it into the Eleventh Five Year Plan (2007–2012).

The government has also provided incentives for Export Oriented Units (EOUs) including tax exemption on export income and no import or export duty. The tax exemption for EOUs has fostered their growth, and there are already 150 EOUs in clusters like Bengaluru.[117] However, the government has decreed that this tax exemption regime will end by 2009. Meanwhile, the government is sanctioning Special Economic Zones (SEZs) that also provide tax holidays and tax exemptions. Unlike the decentralized, spread-out export units, SEZs will also lead to more clustered production with the associated external economy benefits.

The government has also undertaken other initiatives like the SITP and the Integrated Cluster Development Scheme (ICDS). Earlier, there was the Textile Center Infrastructure Development Scheme (TCIDS) for providing roads and water for cluster development. The objective of these schemes is to tackle the problems of fragmentation in the various sectors of the textile value chain and the nonavailability of quality infrastructure.[118] In a nutshell, the aim was to consolidate individual units into clusters and to provide them with world-class infrastructure facilities through public-private partnerships (PPP).

Under the SITP, launched in 2005, 100 acres of land is provided for the construction of each integrated textile park. These are premarketed parks, which would incorporate facilities for spinning, sizing, texturizing, weaving, processing, apparels, and embellishments. The government provides grants, but, prior to that, the investors must come up with a viable plan. The government contributes 40 percent of the project cost, while 60 percent is met by the users. The user groups have to pay 20 percent up front, and 40 percent of the project cost is borrowed from banks. IL&FS, who are the program directors for SITP, help in obtaining these loans.[119] Between 2005–2006 and 2006–2007, project proposals worth Rs. 2.4 billion had been sanctioned, of which government assistance amounted to Rs. 0.8 billion.[120] By 2007, a total of 30 textile parks were approved, out of which two are operational and the rest are expected to be developed by March 2009.[121]

The government also has agrarian schemes that are important for the cotton-based-garment sector. There is enough cotton of the short and medium variety, but not of the long variety, which therefore needs to be imported.[122] While the Indian industry's demand for cotton was expected to grow by 150 percent, it was estimated that only an additional 30 percent could be locally met. The Government thus set up a Technology Mission of Cotton (TMC) in 2003 for technical interventions to increase the production of cotton. The Rs. 6 billion TMC consists of four mini-missions with specific objectives of research, dissemination of technology to farmers, improvement in marketing infrastructure, and modernization of ginning and pressing factories. TMC's research and development activities for high-yielding seeds, including biotechnology and other hybrid seeds, have resulted in a spectacular increase in cotton production and reduction in contamination levels. Cotton yield rose from 300 kg per hectare in 2002 to 470 kg per hectare in 2006, and cotton production rose from 15.8 million bales to 24.4 million bales in the same period.[123]

A cell has been set up in the Ministry of Textiles to attract FDI in textiles, clothing, and machinery. Their Action Plan to attract FDI consists of identifying countries that are strong in certain product segments and targeting technically capable foreign firms and investors to invest in India—either by forging alliances with Indian companies or by investing in fresh capacities in India. India is showcased as an investment destination at international summits, and delegations are sent to prospective investing countries. This cell is also responsible for finding solutions to operational problems, complex administrative procedures, and inadequate infrastructure, transport, and energy.[124]

The government is also helping with skill training of labor by promoting training and vocational institutes. The current training infrastructure consists of engineering colleges, polytechnics, agencies like apparel training and development centers (ATDCs), power looms services centers (PSCs), weaving services centers (WSCs), textiles research associations (TRAs), industrial training institutes (ITIs), and support to private vocational training institutes. However, the output of trainees from the entire existing training infrastructure is not adequate to meet even existing requirements, let alone future needs.

The government is emphasizing the expansion of the current infrastructure of ITIs and polytechnics targeted specifically at the garment sector with the Centers of Excellence Scheme. The ITIs and polytechnics situated near "catchment" areas for the textiles workforce are to include textile/garment-related courses in the instruction. New ITIs will be set up in those areas from where textile workers traditionally migrate but that do not have such institutes. PPPs are being promoted for setting up training centers. The private sector manufacturers with in-house training facilities or trainers are being encouraged to set up training institutes for the RMG sector with government support and a one-time capital grant.[125] The Apparel Export

Promotion Council (AEPC) is running 13 apparel training and design centers (ATDCs), and it plans to set up 25 new centers in 13 states over the next five years.[126]

4.4.4.2. Labor Laws

While the government has provided schemes and initiatives to boost the industry and has liberalized to a certain extent, there is a long list of regulations that entrepreneurs feel hinder the growth of the industry. The RMG sector being labor intensive, the manufacturers' main objection is against the rigid labor laws that do not allow firms to hire workers on contract or hire them for a certain period. Businesses claim that the rigid labor laws are proving to be a bottleneck, particularly for the clothing and apparel sector. Large seasonal orders cannot be taken because the labor strength cannot be reduced during the slack season. Unlike Chinese firms, Indian companies are unable to hire and fire on the basis of such seasonal requirements of this sector. This means that if an order needs 2,000 more people for a short period of four or five months, but there is no confirmed order following that period, the firm is stuck with 2,000 extra people. Firms can hire, but cannot fire. Under the Industrial Disputes Act, 1956, any unit employing over 100 people must obtain necessary approval for layoffs.[127] This has proved to be a hindrance, especially for medium- and large-sized enterprises, as firms can send workers away only with prior permission from the government and that is difficult to obtain (without bribes). Employers have suggested an amendment to the Industrial Disputes Act, asking for raising the upper limit for exemption from the act from the present 100 employees to 500. They also suggested that workforce adjustments (in line with the ILO Convention on Termination of Employment) by the employer due to structural and other changes should be permitted.

Employers have demanded liberalization of labor laws to permit the use of contract labor in EOUs, since the export business in particular is seasonal and contractual in nature. One suggestion is that Section 10 of the Contract Labor (Regulation and Abolition) Act, 1970, should be amended to exclude textile units engaged in export-related activity (where exports comprise 50 percent of their total sales) to facilitate outsourcing activities.

Another employer proposal is to tackle the problem of labor shortage via extension of the government's National Rural Employment Guarantee Act (NREGA) from the construction of rural roads to the garment sector. Under the current NREGA program, employment is provided for 250 days for Rs. 60 a day per worker. The TEA and other garment export associations have been lobbying for the extension of the NREGA to the garment sector, with a provision of a higher daily wage of Rs. 70 a day.[128] This proposal would increase employment while helping the garment industry overcome the labor shortage.

There is also an upper limit of 2,000 on the number of workers in each factory, which can be increased only by special approval from the government. This means that if a firm employs 10,000 workers, they must be spread over five factories of 2,000 workers each. This has led to the fragmentation of the industry and the fragmentation has prevented the firms from benefiting from economies of scale. Indian firms require several units to be set up separately, whereas an Indonesian or Chinese company would typically have two or three units. This hinders investment and rationalization of the workforce and limits flexibility.

In labor-intensive sectors of the textile industry, such as garments, the limit of nine hours a shift and 48 hours a week is perceived as another limitation. It restrains firms from catering to peak season requirements of customers and compensating for low labor productivity. There has been a demand from industry that working hours should be increased to 12 hours a shift and 60 hours a week, with due compensation, in certain labor-intensive segments.[129] As of now, one can run 60 hours by getting permission from the Labor Commission and the process allegedly is not straightforward.[130] Such labor market restrictions are believed to have deterred FDI in India, particularly firms interested in large units.

Certain state governments, like Karnataka, have changed rules to help out the industry. Women workers in Karnataka were earlier only allowed to work till 6 p.m. and this limit was extended to 10 p.m.[131] The extension has made a huge difference to the garment industries in the Bengaluru cluster area, since, as earlier pointed out, the majority of workers in the RMG sector are women.

Summary and Recommendations

The year following the MFA phaseout saw the RMG sector's exports grow by 31.2 percent. A confluence of policy, environment, and individual and collective initiatives led to this success. After the dismantling of the MFA, India has benefited due to raw material, design skills, and labor advantages and also due to a large vertically integrated production structure. Based on long experience, firms explored the international market and forged strategic partnerships internally and with international buyers and suppliers.

The main stumbling blocks are the rigid labor laws and the reservations of the industry for the SSI sector. However, the latter has been used to the industry's advantage, since the small-scale production enabled drawing on traditional styles and combining these with modern marketing knowledge to develop niche markets. Thus RMG firms have used the fragmentation of the Indian textile sector to their advantage by developing flexibility for product diversification and capturing niche markets in stylized, medium-end, and low-volume products. Indian firms have grasped the importance of brands, and by making a headway toward creating brands, they have moved up the value chain. Business leaders also invest a great deal in traveling to explore the market and establish business networks.

At the other end of the scale, collaboration within clusters, such as Tirupur, has enabled firms to benefit from synergies and other cluster-related external economies. Innovative joint action within clusters includes the joint use of capacity, joint training, and collaboration to win contracts, the benefits of which are shared. The increasing sophistication of the sector is evident from its collaboration with other industries to develop, using nano-technology, new products, such as "wrinkle-free" trousers, and to market them. The Indian garment sector has become the engine for growth of the whole textile value chain.

The government has also instituted a range of enabling policies such as duty/tax reimbursement schemes, interest rate subsidies, schemes for better supply of raw material, modernization, technological upgrading, and cluster development. Government support has helped mitigate the supply-side constraints faced by Indian companies such as low productivity, poor infra-structure, high costs of inputs and technology, and limited access to finance. Although the government's regulatory barriers and labor laws continue to be hindrances, institutional support and investment have played a role in helping RMG firms achieve competitiveness.

Enhanced efficiency and productivity are a must for Indian firms to meet the emerging challenge of global competition in the post-MFA era. Investment, technological and infrastructural upgrading, and labor market rigidities are some of the key issues that need to be addressed for the RMG sector to con-tinue on its trajectory of high growth. To remain competitive in the interna-tional market, the Indian government needs to ensure large investments in improvement of technology and in infrastructure by scaling up schemes like TUFS and SITP. There has been a growing demand from entrepreneurs to increase the cap on the TUFS scheme to Rs. 20 million per unit, which is under consideration by the government. The government should also provide incentives for domestic manufacturing of machinery to increase the availabil-ity of indigenous capital goods at a lower price for different segments of the textile industry. This is a backward linkage that needs more attention.

However, in spite of a supportive policy environment, the flow of FDI in the garment sector is restricted due to stringent labor laws and regulatory barriers. FDI would benefit the industry not only financially, but also in terms of technology transfer, quality enhancement, marketing support, and creation of large scale facilities. The Indian government should exploit the current attractiveness of the country to FDI and encourage joint ventures by reforming the country's infrastructure and lowering logistics and regulatory hurdles. Most importantly, it could make labor laws more flexible, with due remuneration for labor and in consistency with ILO regulations, to make it favorable for investors to enter the labor-intensive textile industry.

RMG entrepreneurs want flexible labor laws that permit the hiring of contract labor, since the export business in particular is seasonal and contractual in nature. Employers argue that since there is a shortage of skilled labor, they are unlikely to invest in training contract labor only to lose them. Thus, firms have an incentive in retaining trained workers for future needs, even if they are hired on contract basis. It is also in the firms' interest to ensure the health, safety, welfare, and social security of workers, which are in any case required by the social compliance standards imposed and audited by foreign buyers. The extension of NREGA from construction of rural roads to the garment sector has been proposed by employers to ease the labor shortage.

The export-intensive, cotton-based Indian RMG sector has witnessed tremendous growth in recent years, which can be attributed to its many strengths, strategies, and synergies. While the Indian RMG sector is the best performer in South Asia, the resolution of hurdles to investment and efficiency is crucial for the sustenance of its high growth in an increasingly competitive market.

Annexure 4.1

List of Interviewees in India

1. Mr. A. Sakthivel, Chairman, Poppys Group, and President, Tirupur Exporters Association.
2. Mr. Hemchandra Javeri, President, Madura Garments, Bengaluru.
3. Mr. Rahul Mehta, Managing Director, Creative Outwear Ltd., Mumbai, and President, Clothing Manufacturers' Association of India.
4. Mr. D. K. Nair, Secretary General, Confederation of Indian Textile Industry (CITI), Delhi.
5. Mr. Vivek Hinduja, CEO Marketing, Gokaldas Exports, Bengaluru.
6. Sriram Srinivasan, Head, Reliance Retail Apparel Business, Mumbai.
7. Mr. Partho Kar, CEO, Madura Garments.
8. Mr. D. L. Sharma, President, Vardhaman Textiles Ltd.
9. Mr. R. C. M. Reddy, Director, Cluster Development Initiative, IL&FS.

10. Mr. R. C. Jhamtani, Former Sr. Adviser (Industry), Planning Commission.
11. Mr. S. N. Dash, Adviser (Industry), Planning Commission.
12. Mr. Jagadish Hinduja, Managing Director, Gokaldas Images, Yeshwantpur, Bengaluru.
13. Mr. P. Shanmugam, Director, The Great Indian Linen and Textile Company Ltd., Coimbatore.
14. Mr. B. S. Sinha, Director, Cotton Division, Ministry of Textiles.
15. Mr. Goldy Puri, Managing Director, Marshal Overseas Pvt. Ltd., Noida, National Capital Region.
16. Mr. Sudha Anand, Director, BKS Textiles Private Ltd., Palladam.
17. Mr. Kesar, Director, Okhla Garment and Textiles Cluster (OGTC), New Delhi.
18. Mr. Gunish Jain, Director, Royal Embroidery, and Member, OGTC, New Delhi.
19. Mr. Narahari, Chief of Marketing, Madura Garments, Bengaluru.
20. Mr. A. C. Khullar, Director (Textiles), Planning Commission.
21 Mr. M. S. Ramananda, Senior Manager (Exports), K. Mohan & Company Pvt. Ltd., Bengaluru.
22. Mrs. Asha Dhar, Manager, Indo Polycoats Ltd., New Delhi.
23. Mr. S. G. Raoot, Joint Adviser (Village and Small Enterprises), Planning Commission.
24. Mr. K. Ajay Narayanan, Sr. Manager (Exports), Alok Industries Ltd., Mumbai.
25. Mr. R. M. Subramaniam, Consultant, Cluster Devt Initiative, IL&FS, Palladam.
26. Mr. S. Hariharan, General Manager, Sonal Garments, Bengaluru.
27. Mr. Senthil Kumar, Divisional Manager, Sonal Garments, Bengaluru.
28. Mr. R. Dhamotharan, Category Head (innerwear, outerwear, and knit-wear), Madura Garments, Bengaluru.
29. Ms. Meera, Manager, Cascade Enterprises.
30. Ms. Sheetal Jambhale, Merchandiser, Alok Industries Ltd. Mumbai.
31. Mr. Narendra, Director, Indus Fila, Yashwantpur, Bengaluru.

CHAPTER 5

The Readymade Garment Sector in Nepal

5.1. Introduction

At the beginning of the study, following the procedure outlined in chapter 1, two products from the RMG sector were selected for Nepal, based on the criteria of high export growth rate and high volume of exports.[1] As in the chapters on other countries in this volume, the original study plan here too was to delve into processes, including linkages and partnerships, to explain the reason for the export success of these two products. However, preliminary fieldwork indicated a dramatically different situation on the ground relative to the trend indicated by the secondary UN data over the past decade (1994–2003).[2] With the phaseout of the quota system under the MFA, the RMG sector was unraveling in Nepal. Only 99 garment factories remained registered in 2006, compared to a peak of 234 in 1990–1991, out of which barely 25 were operational. The share of RMG sector in exports had also declined from over 25 percent throughout the 1990s to about 10 percent in 2005. The RMG sector could not be characterized as a "success," as will be explained in this chapter.

The central question in this case study was modified not only to understand the reasons for Nepal's initial success in the RMG sector, but also to find out why this sector failed to survive, when it thrived, in varying degrees, in the other South Asian countries in our study. The role of the government, RMG entrepreneurs, supply-side constraints, and demand-side factors are examined to identify the reasons for the emergence and decline of the RMG sector in Nepal.

Section 2 provides an overview of Nepal's RMG sector with a focus on exports; section 3 highlights in general terms, drawing on secondary data, the emergence and slow decline of the sector; and section 4 continues this discussion using the findings of our survey of entrepreneurs. Section 5 addresses the role of government and section 6 that of entrepreneurs.

5.2. Sector Trade Background

Despite the adoption of export-diversification policies since the mid-1980s, over 60 percent of Nepal's exports went to India, mostly primary goods. Woolen carpets, RMG, and pashmina (type of cashmere wool and textiles made from it) emerged as major exports in the early 1990s, contributing to over two-thirds of Nepal's non-Indian exports. Thus, these items not only diversified Nepal's exports from primary to manufactured products but also helped ease Nepal's trade dependence on India.

The United States, Canada, European Union, Japan, and India are the major destinations for the Nepali apparel sector as shown in Table 5.1.

The United States has been the prime market for Nepali apparel exports with a share of almost 91 percent in 2000–2001. While the United States' share steadily declined to 62 percent, the European Union increased its share to about 27 percent of Nepal's total RMG exports in 2005–2006. Japan and Canada also picked up some of the export decline to the USA. RMG exports to India increased but remained modest on both absolute and relative scales, despite market proximity and a bilateral preferential trading arrangement between the two countries.

Low-end cotton apparels dominated Nepal's RMG exports, especially to the United States. But in the European market, Nepal managed to export high-value wool and silk-based items. Table 5.2 provides details of the five major Nepali RMG exports to the United States and the European Union.

Table 5.3 demonstrates that the concentration of exports in any one country was higher for Nepal than for the other countries in South Asia.

Table 5.1 Share of major markets for Nepal's RMG exports (percentages)

Year	United States	European Union	Canada	Japan
2000–2001	90.96	7.32	0.91	0.42
2001–2002	85.28	12.28	0.85	0.60
2002–2003	87.87	9.80	1.00	0.65
2003–2004	75.58	20.48	2.18	1.00
2004–2005	75.18	17.84	3.25	1.45
2005–2006*	62.07	27.31	3.58	2.00

NA: not available.
* First ten months.
Source: Adhikari (2006), SWATEE/ActionAid (Table 3.9, p. 21).

Table 5.2 Five major Nepali RMG items exported to the United States and European Union (Nepali Rupees, NPR)

United States			European Union		
	Export value			Export value	
Product	2003–2004	2004–2005	Product	2003–2004	2004–2005
Cotton trousers and shorts for men/boys	862,952,292	752,731,557 (−12.77)	Woolen or fine animal-hair shawls, scarves, and veils	555,072,861	564,607,861 (1.71)
Cotton T-shirts, singlets, and other vests	798,928,706	29,362,547 (−96.32)	Cotton trousers and shorts for women/girls	320,025,802	102,088,423 (−68.09)
Cotton blouses and shirts for women/girls	574,362,841	212,955,259 (−62.92)	Cotton blouses and shirts for women/girls	198,771,131	65,345,078 (−67.12)
Cotton trousers and shorts for women/girls	561,197,763	324,827,056 (−3.49)	Cotton pullovers, cardigans, and similar articles	26,721,598	62,043,884 (132.18)
Cotton pullovers, cardigans, and similar articles	336,590,606	324,827,056 (−3.49)	Silk shawls, scarves, and veils	906,794	33,532,562 (3,601)

Figures in parentheses denote export growth rate.
Source: SAWTEE (2006).

Table 5.3 Share of the United States and European Union in the total RMG exports of South Asian countries

	Major export market (% exports)	
Country	United States	European Union
Bangladesh (2002)	38	56
India (2004)	24	33
Nepal (2004)	80	18
Pakistan (2004)	31	32
Sri Lanka (2005)	57	35

Source: Adhikari (2006).

Table 5.4 Contribution of RMG sector to Nepal's total exports (million NPRs)

Year	Total exports	RMG exports	RMG share in total exports
1993–1994	19,293.4	5,943.2	30.8
1994–1995	17,639.2	5,139.3	29.1
1995–1996	19,881.1	5,374.8	27.0
1996–1997	22,636.5	5,955	26.3
1997–1998	27,513.5	7,032.5	25.6
1998–1999	35,676.3	9,744.7	27.3
1999–2000	49,822.7	13,987.7	28.1
2000–2001	55,654.1	13,316.8	23.9
2001–2002	46,944.8	8,046.5	17.1
2002–2003	49,930.6	12,289.3	24.6
2003–2004	53,910.7	10,176.7	18.9
2004–2005	58,705.7	6,490.5	11.1
2005–2006*	55,812.5	6,505.7	11.7

* For the first eleven months only. The value of the Nepali rupee (NPR) relative to the dollar and euro in July 2004 was Rs. 75 and Rs. 92, respectively.
Source: Economic Survey, Ministry of Finance (various issues).

5.3. Rise and Decline of the RMG Sector

5.3.1. *The Initial Success*

The share of RMG sector in total exports grew steadily from less than 1 percent in 1980, and it became Nepal's largest manufacturing sector between 1990 and 2000. As indicated in Table 5.4, RMG's share in total exports rose to 31 percent in 1993–1994. However, it began to fall from that year (almost steadily, with very few exceptions) to 11 percent in 2004–2005.

The RMG sector has been important for the Nepali economy in terms of its contribution toward employment and exports. In 1981, manufacturing accounted for only 0.5 percent of total employment. The emergence of the RMG sector along with an increase in carpets and pashmina exports led to an increase in the share of employment generated by the manufacturing industry to 8.8 percent in 2001. By 1999–2000, the RMG sector provided direct employment to over 50,000 unskilled workers and accounted for about 12 percent of employment in the manufacturing sector.[3] According to a survey by South Asian Watch on Trade, Economics, and Environment (SAWTEE), about 45 percent of the workers of this sector were women.[4]

5.3.2. The Decline

The Nepali RMG sector declined through the 1990s and more rapidly after 2001. In 2001, 212 firms were in operation, and in 2004, there were 138 firms. By 2006, only 99 firms remained registered, out of which barely 20 firms were in operation.[5] Despite the decline in establishments, the output and the average number of employees per establishment continued to rise, signaling a trend toward larger establishments. In 1991–1992, the average number of employees per establishment was 74 and this increased to 109 in 1996–1997 and to 158 in 2001–2002.

The contribution of the RMG sector to total manufacturing declined from around 37 percent in 1994–1995 to 26 percent in 2003–2004 and to 16 percent in 2004–2005.[6] Corresponding to the decline in the number of firms, the RMG sector also witnessed a decline in exports. RMG exports almost halved from NPR 12.3 billion in 2002–2003 to NPR 6.5 billion in 2004–2005 (Table 5.4). The share of RMGs in total exports declined from 27 percent in 1995–1996 to about 12 percent in 2005–2006. During 1991–1995, the RMG sector had witnessed high growth rates of about 29 percent, but during 2001–2005, growth was a negative 15 percent.[7]

As indicated above, the RMG sector had played a key role with regards to employment and exports, and so this sector's decline had predictable negative effects on Nepal's economy and forced it to once again depend on India. Of the 50,000 workers employed by the sector in 1999–2000, only 5,000 remained in 2005–2006—a ten-fold decline. About 60 percent of the retrenchment occurred in the two years after the MFA phaseout, or almost 80 percent of it since 2002.[8] As evident from Table 5.4, the downward trend preceded the MFA phaseout, though the latter appears to have accelerated the decline. This decline is also evident from data collected from sources in importing countries (see Table 2.3, Annexures 2.2, 2.3).

Unemployment especially increased among women, as they are usually the first to be laid off during labor cuts.[9] In addition, it is difficult for laid-off workers to find employment in other sectors due to the lack of transferable skills.

5.4. Survey Findings

This section reports findings based on a survey of RMG entrepreneurs in Kathmandu. Following the pattern established in section 5.3 above, we first examine the reasons for the emergence of the RMG sector in Nepal, before turning to the causes of its decline.

5.4.1. Reasons for the Emergence of RMG Sector in Nepal

Our survey findings reveal that an interplay of domestic and international factors led to the rapid growth of the RMG sector in Nepal. Nepal had been undergoing a slow structural change; the share of agriculture in GDP had declined continuously from 61.3 percent in 1975 to 41.7 percent in 1995 to 39.2 percent in 2005.[10] However, notwithstanding this change in the structure of the economy, Nepal's labor market had lagged. As mentioned earlier, the contribution of the manufacturing sector to total employment was only 8.8 percent in 2001. Unemployment was high, and a majority of unskilled labor was yet to be absorbed into the economy. Due to the availability of abundant labor, Nepal's comparative advantage in the labor-intensive RMG sector was self-evident. In such a scenario, the international quota-based system in RMG trade under the MFA provided the trigger for the initiation of RMG manufacturing in Nepal.

The MFA framework provided market access to a large number of developing countries, and Nepal also emerged as a relocation site, especially for Indian producers who had been constrained by the MFA quota ceilings. They began pouring into Nepal to evade the quotas during the late 1970s. The export-oriented industries were initially dominated by Indian manufacturers, who had experience and knowledge of the supply chain of RMG exports. After gaining experience from Indian entrepreneurs, Nepalese entrepreneurs started their own factories. Until 1996, the total quotas of Nepal in RMG exports were equally divided between the registered garment factories. This lowered entry barriers and encouraged the establishment of new garment factories. Since RMG production required relatively low-capital investment, it led to an unprecedented growth of the industry. As the United States was a major quota-imposing country, a majority of Nepali entrepreneurs began to concentrate on the U.S. market.

The role of the government in the initiation of the RMG sector in Nepal can be described as neutral. The sector has benefited and continues to receive government benefits that are applicable to any other export-oriented industry. However, no additional benefits or incentives were provided by the government to attract investment into this sector.

5.4.2. Reasons for the Decline

A number of developing countries had entered the international RMG market under the quota system. After the phaseout of the MFA, a number of these countries, including Nepal and all the other South Asian countries, continued to maintain or enhance their exports share in the U.S. and EU markets (Table 2.3). According to our survey, apart from the phaseout of the MFA, the other reasons for the decline of the RMG sector in Nepal include political instability, labor relations, lack of backward and forward linkages, structural constraints (landlocked), and the country's inability to assume a more central role in the supply chain. The subsections below will examine each of these issues.

5.4.2.1. The Phaseout of the MFA

The phaseout of the quota system created winners and losers among the low- and medium-income countries. Unfortunately, Nepal was one of the biggest losers. As Table 5.5 reveals, while other South Asian countries, except the Maldives, managed to not only retain but improve their market share, Nepal's RMG exports shrank by 46 percent and saw a decline of 26 percent in revenue.[11]

In the case of the European Union, Canada, and Japan, due to the preferential market access granted by these countries to Nepal under the Generalized System of Preferences (GSP), exports continued to rise. Since

Table 5.5 Change in RMG exports in selected Asian countries following the MFA phaseout

| | Million US$ | | | Million sq.m. equivalent | | |
| | January–September | | | January–September | | |
Countries	2004	2005	% change	2004	2005	% change
Bangladesh	1,546.7	1,839.6	18.9	835	1,000.6	19.8
China	1,0907.3	1,7591.2	61.3	8,717.8	12,727.9	46.0
India	2,764.5	3,473	25.6	1,460.1	1,756	20.3
Pakistan	1,908.0	2,130	11.6	2,261.2	2,433.1	7.6
Sri Lanka	1,151.6	1,274.3	10.7	366.8	397.0	8.2
Cambodia	1,076.6	1,263	17.3	502.5	541.4	7.7
Nepal	103.1	76	−26.3	33.9	18.3	−46.0

Source: OTEXA, Department of Commerce, United States and SAWTEE (2006).

the quota phaseout was gradual, over ten years, until the completion of the phaseout, the export value of RMG exports from Nepal was not seriously affected due to the "back-loading" or delay in eliminating quotas on product categories that were of interest to Nepal.

After the phaseout, the negative impact on Nepalese exports was compounded by United States' tariff concession to the Caribbean and South American countries under the North American Free Trade Association (NAFTA), Caribbean Basin Trade Partnership Act (CBTPA), and Central American Free Trade Association (CAFTA). In addition, the United States also provides duty-free access to economically vulnerable African countries under the African Growth and Opportunity Act (AGOA). As the United States was the major market destination for Nepali exports, these trade agreements had a disproportionate negative impact on Nepal.

5.4.2.2. Lack of Political Stability
According to the entrepreneurs in the survey, apart from the quota phaseout, lack of political stability is one of the most important factors for the decline of the RMG sector. This occurred due to a decade-long conflict between the government and Maoist insurgents. The strikes and shutdowns organized by various political parties and ethnic groups also had a detrimental effect on production. They interfered with the delivery of raw materials, a majority of which were imported. Since the lead time is important in the international RMG trade, the delays in shipping orders caused by such political instability resulted in loss of market share, which was difficult to recoup once captured by competitors.[12]

5.4.2.3. Labor Relations
Labor relations in Nepal have not been cordial. According to the World Bank (2006), Nepal is one of the most difficult countries in the world for employers to hire and fire workers. Table 5.6 compares various indicators of

Table 5.6   Labor market rigidity in Nepal

Indicators	Nepal	Region	OECD
Difficulty of hiring index	67.0	41.8	27.0
Rigidity of hours index	20.0	25.0	45.2
Difficulty of firing index	70.0	37.5	27.4
Rigidity of employment index	52.0	34.8	33.3
Hiring cost (% of salary)	10.0	6.8	21.4
Firing costs (weeks of wages)	90.0	71.5	31.3

Source: World Bank (2006).

employment in Nepal with those of other countries in the region and OECD countries. Each index is assigned values between 0 and 100, with higher values representing more rigid work conditions. The rigidity of the employment index is an average of three subindices. Nepal has a high score of 67 for difficulty of hiring index and a score of 70 for difficultly of firing index, indicating rigid rules and regulations for hiring and firing workers. Similarly, other measures of labor market rigidity, such as firing costs (weeks of wages), are also higher than the regional average as indicated in Table 5.6.

The overall score for rigidity of employment index at 52 was much higher than the average score of 34.8 for the region and 33.3 for OECD countries. For a country with high unemployment, achieving a balance between providing social security to the workers and encouraging the private sector with labor market flexibility is difficult. Our bias is toward labor protection, but we think that the state could initiate welfare measures on its own rather than impose rules on companies.

Labor disputes appear to be among the most important reasons for the decline of the RMG sector in Nepal. As indicated earlier, labor disputes seriously affect timely delivery of consignments, making it impossible for entrepreneurs to compete in the international RMG market.[13]

5.4.2.4. Nepal as a Landlocked Country

Due to Nepal's landlocked geographical setting, the country's major trade routes depend on access to India's transportation system. As 90 percent of the export goods pass through India, Nepal's exports incur transportation costs that are about 20 percent higher than those incurred by other RMG exporters in the region. In addition, Nepali RMG exporters also have to bear the full cost of container and clearance charges in Kolkata, regardless of the volume of the goods, which further raises the transportation cost. Naturally, the high cost of transportation and associated logistics increases the overall cost of production and makes it difficult for Nepal to compete internationally.

Furthermore, Nepal's geographical constraints increase delivery time and bureaucratic hassles for traders. Under the Treaty of Transit with India, exporters need four documents to transfer goods from the Kolkata port into Nepal. On the domestic side, the amount of paperwork formalities averages 11 for exporters and 15 for importers.[14] Currently, it takes Nepali exporters three to five days to facilitate the transit of goods from Kolkata. Similarly, inspection at custom points, which is done on all the containers rather than on a sample basis, often causes delays. It is estimated that the delivery time for Nepali RMG suppliers is 50 percent longer than for other suppliers in the region.[15] Since the trend in international clothing industry is toward substantially declining lead times, this long delivery time poses a serious challenge to Nepal's ability to remain competitive.[16]

5.5. Role of the Government

Despite liberalization, the government can still play an important role in the economy through an active industrial policy. Given Nepal's status as among the least developed countries, WTO trade rules allow it considerable policy space.[17] Government support can range from creating a favorable industrial policy environment for private investment to promoting specific sectors/industries through tax incentives, subsidies, and duty-draw-back schemes. Various low- and middle-income countries, including other South Asian countries, have implemented measures to support their RMG sector, especially after the quota phaseout, as reported in the other chapters of this book. These measures include post-MFA preparations, such as training displaced workers to make them eligible for alternative jobs (Bangladesh), measures to reduce lead time (Bangladesh, China, India), funds for upgrading technology (Bangladesh, China, India, Indonesia, Pakistan, Sri Lanka), encouraging backward linkages (Vietnam, Sri Lanka, Bangladesh, China, India), tax incentives (Bangladesh, China, India, Indonesia, Pakistan, Sri Lanka, Vietnam), and other measures to bolster competitiveness.[18]

Despite the importance of the RMG sector for Nepal's exports and for employment, the industry does not enjoy any added incentives from the government. RMG entrepreneurs stressed the importance of a garment processing zone (GPZ) and the need for the state to lobby for market access.

In 2001, the Garment Association of Nepal (GAN) suggested the establishment of a GPZ to develop a cluster of garment factories with all ancillary industries and logistic services. The GPZ would be crucial to facilitate the horizontal and vertical integration of the RMG sector and would lead to economies of scale. Nepali garment entrepreneurs wanted the establishment of the GPZ closer to the Inland Container Depots (ICD) at Birgunj to facilitate efficient delivery. Even though the government committed to developing a GPZ several years ago, this facility is yet to materialize. An SEZ was proposed in the budget speech for fiscal year 2006–2007, and the SEZ, currently under construction in Bhairahawa, is expected to be operational in a year. However, garment entrepreneurs are sceptical of its usefulness to help revive garment exports and are still insisting on a GPZ at Birgunj.

Much of the problems in transportation and delivery faced by Nepali exporters could be reduced by enhancing the facilities and management of the ICD in Nepal.[19] It is estimated that transportation costs in the garment sector could be reduced by 40 percent if the ICD facilities are fully utilized.[20] Thus, establishment of a GPZ at Birgunj and proper utilisation of the ICD facility could not only reduce the transportation and logistics costs but also improve the delivery time of RMG exports.

As indicated in Table 5.1, the Nepali RMG sector is highly concentrated on the U.S. market; the United States accounted for about 62 percent of Nepal's exports in 2005–2006. Nepalese apparels are subject to average tariffs of about 15 percent in the United States, which is almost ten times greater than the United States' average MFN rate for other products.[21] Unlike other major RMG-importing countries, such as the European Union and Canada, the United States has not provided duty-free access to products from least developed countries (LDCs). The garment entrepreneurs, and especially the GAN, have been urging the government to lobby for duty-free access to the United States, by allying with other LDCs, through the Tariff Relief Act for Developing Economies (TRADE). The proposed TRADE Act, if implemented, would eliminate U.S. tariffs on a wide range of imports, including textiles and apparel, from 14 of the world's LDCs—Afghanistan, Bangladesh, Bhutan, Cambodia, East Timor, Kiribati, Laos, Maldives, Nepal, Samoa, Solomon Islands, Tuvalu, Vanuatu, and Yemen. The legislation is designed to spur growth in some of the poorest nations of the world by increasing their access to the U.S. market.

5.6. Role of Entrepreneurs

The nature of clothing trade has changed from purely cut-make-trim (C-M-T) to a more service-oriented business. Unlike in the past, manufacturers now are responsible for an integrated production network consisting of all activities from sourcing of raw materials to production, marketing, and distribution. Price advantage alone is not sufficient to compete in the international market; manufacturers have to consider the quality, reliability, transport and transaction, and other costs as important variables in order to be competitive.

In this context, the competitiveness of Nepali manufacturers also depends on whether they can manage the supply chains efficiently. They need to be able to meet the international RMG market's required lead time, which has reduced tremendously over the years. The average time (from design stage to the distribution center in United States) for orders for one major buyer came down from 21 weeks in 2000 to 12 weeks in 2003.[22]

Most of the RMG manufacturing in Nepal is still limited to C-M-T, while sourcing materials, design, and market research is done by the international buyers themselves. Nepali RMG entrepreneurs claim that they have neither the economic resources nor in-depth knowledge about the international fashion industry to conduct independent market research. In addition, most RMG manufacturers do not have direct contact with the international buyers and are limited to subcontracting orders from India.

Most of the raw materials and accessories (fabric, buttons, thread) for the RMG sector are also not yet made in Nepal but imported from China, India, and other countries. Entrepreneurs think that backward linkages in the RMG sector are weak due to the lack of economies of scale and greater capital requirements. The inability of Nepali RMG entrepreneurs to move up the value chain by establishing direct links with international buyers has limited Nepal's role to that of a supplier of cheap labor—easily substitutable by other competitors.

Although generally characterized as labor-intensive, the Nepali RMG sector has a higher capital-labor ratio than competitor countries, as indicated in Table 5.7.

The capital-labor ratio in Nepal is about seven times higher than in India, five times higher than in Vietnam, and over three times higher than in China. This is suggestive of a higher import burden for Nepal since the machinery is imported. It also suggests that the Nepali RMG sector has been unable to fully utilize cheap labor to benefit from the lower-cost advantage. One of the reasons for lower labor content in value added is that products made in Nepal are mechanized lower-end commodities rather than high-value fashion items that require high-value inputs of skilled manpower.

In such a scenario, it is important for Nepali RMG entrepreneurs not only to diversify their exports to countries other than the United States, but also to diversify into higher value-added items to fully utilize the labor advantage. However, despite the stepwise phaseout of the MFA, Nepali entrepreneurs seem to have done very little preparation to survive in the postquota era.

Table 5.7   Decomposition of value added* in the RMG sector in selected countries (% of gross input)

	Labor	Capital	Capital-labor ratio	Value added
Nepal	13.8	27.7	2.0	41.5
Vietnam	10.2	3.8	0.4	14.0
India	24.0	7.8	0.3	31.8
China	20.7	12.2	0.6	32.9

* Value added is defined as total revenue minus intermediate input costs. Hence it generally represents the contribution of labor and capital to production.
Source: SAWTEE (2006) and Nordus (2004).

As indicated in Table 5.1, the market destinations for the Nepali RMG sector where it has high growth potential are the European Union and India, and to a lesser extent Canada and Japan. Their share in Nepal's exports correspondingly increased as that of the United States declined between 2000–2001 and 2005–2006. Nepali exports to the European Union consist of high-value wool and silk-based items and some cotton products. The EU market assumes particular importance given the quota-free access it provides to LDCs like Nepal through the GSP. In addition, the stringent ROOs have also been temporarily waived for Nepal.[23]

India is also a growing market for Nepali RMG exports. India accounts for over one-fifth of the world's population and has a rising middle class, and so this market is expected to assume even greater importance with the booming Indian economy. Owing to Nepal's historic economic and social links with India and its landlocked geography, Nepal already has strong traditional trade relations with India. Given the proximity, Nepali entrepreneurs have a delivery time advantage, especially if the government manages to construct the GPZ. In addition, Nepal also has the advantage of preferential market access to India through the Indo-Nepal bilateral treaty. Nepal can also attract spill-over RMG business from India, as the cost of production and inputs in India has gradually increased. However, despite the proximity advantage, relatively lower labor costs, and preferential market access, India still accounts for a tiny share in Nepal's RMG exports (less than 6 percent in 2005–2006), and this is also an opportunity Nepalese entrepreneurs need to take advantage of.

Conclusion and Recommendations

The RMG sector in Nepal emerged due to the MFA quotas that had become a constraint for Indian manufacturers. With the ready supply of unskilled labor in Nepal, Indian manufacturers relocated their units to Nepal, stimulating the growth of the RMG sector there. Nepalese entrepreneurs soon learned the trade and started their own operations. The equal sharing of quotas by the Nepalese government along with the low-capital requirements in RMG production led to a rapid growth of the sector. Other than the quota allocations provided by the government on an equitable basis, no special incentives were provided for this sector.

The RMG sector came to play a prominent role in the Nepalese economy in terms of value added, employment, and exports. It contributed significantly to the growth of the manufacturing sector, which until then had been very small, and to the diversification of its export base, which until then had been mostly limited to the export of primary goods to India. It also made a major contribution to the employment of women.

The sector's decline began even before the MFA phaseout was complete, and accelerated after that. Our survey of exporters indicates the reasons why Nepal was unable to retain market share after the MFA phaseout, unlike other South Asian countries such as Bangladesh, India, Pakistan, and Sri Lanka. The United States was Nepal's main export market. The free-trade agreements between the United States and other economies in South and Central America and trade concessions for Africa therefore made Nepal more vulnerable to a loss of market share. In addition, political instability and labor unrest took their toll. In a highly competitive environment, lost market share due to tardy delivery or nondelivery is very difficult to recoup.

Another factor specific to Nepal in the subcontinent is its landlocked status. This means that its exporters have to depend on transit via India and incur much higher transportation and logistical costs than those in the rest of the region. It also increases transaction time, since both imports and exports are subject to a number of bureaucratic formalities. Not only does this add to transaction costs, it also reduces the ability of Nepali businesses to have full control over delivery, a critical aspect of the RMG trade.

The Government of Nepal has been slow to institute an industrial policy to address these problems, and this is also specific to Nepal, notwithstanding the complaints by businesses in other South Asian countries. This is despite the fact that Nepal qualifies as a least developed economy member of the WTO and is provided with the requisite policy space. Exporters have complained that the government has been slow in addressing the logistical and trade problems, and in facilitating and rationalizing dry port facilities that would cut transport costs. It has been slow in setting up a GPZ to enhance linkages and economies of scale. Finally, it has been slow in lobbying for an extension of the United States' TRADE Act to Nepal for duty-free garment exports. Given how important the U.S. market remains for Nepal, extension of the Act would provide the time needed by exporters to become more competitive, with the industrial policy assistance of the government.

Nepali entrepreneurs also need to become more assertive. They have not yet established direct links with the buying firms and are still at the bottom end of the value chain, subcontracting orders for India-based firms. They have also not explored backward linkage possibilities, arguing that the capital requirements are too onerous.

Nepalese entrepreneurs have also not taken advantage of the booming Indian economy, despite Nepal's relatively lower labor cost, market proximity, and preferential market access. Nor have they fully utilized the opportunities made available by the European Union, which has waived ROO restrictions for Nepal and has extended Nepal's duty-free export privileges as a least developed country. Even as Nepal lobbies for greater market access in its traditional U.S. market, Nepalese entrepreneurs can take advantage of available markets and upgrade their product range and move up the value chain.

Annexure 5.1

List of Interviewees and Firms in Nepal

1. Evergreen Apparels, Baneshwor, Kathmandu.
2. Cotton Comfort, Sinamangal, Kathmandu.
3. Mahabir Garments, Tripureshwor, Kathmandu.
4. Star Fashion, Harishiddi, Lalitpur.
5. Gaurav Imports, Baneshwor, Kathamandu.
6. Sabnam Garments, Battisputali, Kathmandu.
7. Mr. Navin Dahal, Executive Director, SAWTEE.
8. Mr. Shiv Raj Bhatt, SAWTEE.
9. Mr. Ratnakar Adhikari, UNDP Asia Pacific Regional Centre in Colombo.
10. Ms. Yumiko Yamamoto, UNDP Asia-Pacific Regional Centre in Colombo.
11. Mr. Kiran Sakha, GAN.
12. Mr. Bijendra Shakya, GAN.
13. Dr. Posh Raj Pandey, Member, National Planning Commission, Government of Nepal.

CHAPTER 6

The Readymade Garment Sector in Pakistan

6.1. Introduction

The RMG sector has been one of the most important sectors in Pakistan's textile industry. Spurred by the MFA quota allocation system (refer to endnote 10), the garment sector emerged in the late 1970s and expanded rapidly (Annexure 2.1). It constituted 8.3 percent of total exports in 2005–2006. At the beginning of the MFA phaseout on January 1, 2005, Pakistan's share was 1 percent of the global apparel market.[1]

Garment manufacturing is the largest source of industrial employment in the country (over 700,000 workers), employing mainly men (90 percent) as sewers, with women working in trimming and packing.[2] There were about 5,000 garment units operating in Pakistan in 2005. Of them, 12 percent were large-scale and 88 percent were small or cottage industries. The total installed capacity was 450,000 sewing machines producing 650 million pieces annually. Most of these garment manufacturing units have fewer than 30 stitching machines. There were 400 units with 30 to 50 machines each, and 600 units with 50 to 300 machines.[3]

The production of garments in Pakistan is concentrated mainly in Karachi, Lahore, and Faisalabad. Karachi specializes in both knitwear and woven garments, Lahore in knitwear, and Faisalabad in home textiles. The main marketing focus of Pakistani exporters has been the United States and the European Union, originally the dominant quota markets. The other major importing countries or regions include Canada, the Middle East, and Australia. Most of the Pakistani garment exporters are geared toward supplying department stores and mass-market discount stores, because this market is huge in terms of volume, though prices are low. Only a few garment exporters are able to cater to big brand names or particular fashion labels.[4]

Pakistan has focused on very few product categories, with a strong bias in favor of men's wear, which represented approximately 70 percent of its total RMG exports in the late 1990s. Only 16–18 percent of Pakistan's exports in the 1990s were women's garments. Baby wear is considered to be a specialized niche market and is hence avoided, particularly by the small-scale manufacturing units. At a broad level, the sector can be classified into the knitted garment segment and the woven garment segment. The knitted garments segment dominates the export product mix, but in both segments of the market Pakistan's focus has been on men's garments.[5]

For both the United States and EU markets, the quota utilizations under the MFA reveal that the Pakistani garment sector is highly dependent first on cotton products and second on male garments. Thus, Pakistan specializes in men's woven and knitwear (shirts and trousers), using locally produced cotton. Based on the product selection reported in Table 1.2, this chapter studies the units producing men's/boys' knitted cotton shirts. We first briefly describe the fieldwork, followed by an explanation of the "success" of the garment sector in general and the selected product in particular. We turn next to the role of government in nurturing the industry and the sector, and finally to current and emerging issues facing the RMG sector in Pakistan.

6.2. Fieldwork

The duration of the fieldwork in Pakistan was four months and included interviews with top management officials, agents of textile and garment buying houses, government officials serving in various government-run institutions, such as the Export Promotion Bureau (EPB) of Pakistan.[6] During this period we also interviewed leaders of associations in the garment sector, such as the Pakistan Readymade Garments Technical Training Institute (PRGTTI), Pakistan Readymade Garment Export Association (PRMGEA), Pakistan Knitwear & Sweaters Exporters Association (PKSEA), and individuals in these associations who have represented Pakistan at various WTO and other international conferences and meetings. The breakdown of the interviews is reported in Table 1.2, and the list of interviewees is reported in the Annexure 6.1.

Background information on each garment manufacturing firm and buying house was obtained through the Internet before the scheduled interview. By visiting the company's Web site, information such as the number of employees, range of products, and value of capital stock was acquired ahead of time and only reconfirmed during the interview. This approach was helpful as it gave the interviewer a solid platform to build on and revealed the seriousness and interest of the interviewer to the company's senior management.

The interviews were received warmly and enthusiastically by the interviewees because they saw them as potentially useful for influencing public policy to support the RMG sector with its problems related to post-MFA quota phaseout. The interviewees were eager to supply information about their company or associations and talked freely about their frustrations with government policies. However, as in other case studies, most were reluctant to provide detailed contact information of their foreign partners or buyers.

The research conducted in Karachi was often slowed down by labor and transportation strikes, when all offices and businesses were closed. The month of Ramadan, which in 2006 fell in October,[7] coincided with our research, and not many interviews could be conducted during this month because businesses had shorter working days and because managers were fasting and could not make themselves available.

6.3. Explaining the "Success" of the Textile Industry and the RMG Sector

The emergence of the garment sector in Pakistan, as elsewhere in South Asia, was a result, as predicted by trade theory, of rising unit labor-costs in high-income countries, which made it more competitive to produce RMGs, which are labor-intensive, in low-income countries with lower wages. Thus, as the United States and other Western countries started outsourcing textile and garment production, this whole industry shifted to low-income countries that had cheap labor and other cost advantages, cheap cotton in Pakistan's case.

While this general reasoning applied to Pakistan, the establishment of the RMG sector was also a result of several particular domestic, international, and institutional factors that combined to provide the impetus needed for the growth of this sector. As the world's fourth-largest cotton producer from the early 1970s until 2004–2005 and a possessor of abundant cheap labor, Pakistan was already a major exporter of cotton and cotton yarn.[8] In addition, interviews indicated that the origins of the RMG sector could be attributed to the market opportunity created by the MFA quotas. For example, the supply of local cotton led to a high initial quota allocation for cotton shirts from Pakistan; it had the third-largest quota for the United States in this product category.[9]

Pakistani businesses took advantage of the lack of entry barriers and the low levels of investment required to rapidly move up the value chain. In the late 1970s and early 1980s, as East Asian countries' quotas were fulfilled, buyers began to look to countries like Pakistan. Government policies accelerated this process. Our interviewees suggested that one of the main factors in the growth of the RMG sector was a lucrative rebate on export-related imports offered by the government to garment manufacturers; which in the 1970s was 12–15 percent of the total cost of imports. The government reduced the regulatory duty on polyester chips; waived regulatory duty on industrial sewing machines, knitting machines, and spares; and liberalized the import of textile-processing machinery. The facility of duty-free import of machinery enabled the garments sector to become established and modernized and the technology to be diffused.

Our interviewees suggested that Pakistan was already competitive in the production of cotton. The next logical step was to create forward linkages, which the Pakistani industrialists took, such as investing in spinning yarn, weaving fabric, and establishing a good base in producing knitted shirts, as quotas became available. Establishing a reputation for good quality and timely delivery led to a successful dynamic. Also, internally, the quota system was so structured that companies within the country were able to purchase bigger quotas on the basis of past performance.[10] Thus, over a period, this dynamic resulted in the amassing of considerable quotas for knitted shirts for men and boys by successful exporters, reinforcing their past success.[11] As Table 6.1 indicates, Pakistan was able to build on this initial advantage and was the leading exporter in 2004 in terms of export value and quantity of knit cotton shirts.

As can be seen in Table 6.1, in 2004 Pakistan exported 12.485 million men's/boy's knitted shirts to the United States for a value of $452.43 million, which was higher than the exports of even China and India to the United States in this category. But by 2006, post-MFA, India had already overtaken Pakistan in this product category in value terms.

One may still question why cotton knitted shirts for men and boys emerged as a more successful product than, for example, cotton knitted shirts for women and girls or babies' clothing? The answer lies in the general perceptions and mindset of garment manufacturers coupled with technical difficulties and obstacles in the production process.

Table 6.1 Quantity and value of monthly exports of men's and boys' knit cotton shirts by selected country of origin to the United States

Country	Year	Period (in months)	Quantity	Value ($s)	Unit price ($s)
Pakistan	2006	6	6,285,536	221,660,745	35.26
	2005	12	12,485,360	505,913,082	40.52
	2004	12	9,983,520	452,430,078	45.32
Bangladesh	2006	6	3,207,237	75,543,097	23.55
	2005	12	4,101,102	104,985,441	25.60
	2004	12	1,379,324	55,256,650	40.06
India	2006	6	5,419,125	252,686,993	46.63
	2005	12	8,329,773	412,191,407	49.48
	2004	12	4,539,932	291,261,863	64.16
China	2006	6	1,516,791	85,636,284	56.46
	2005	12	7,980,431	235,602,751	29.52
	2004	12	1,398,664	110,318,238	78.87

Source: Government of Pakistan (2006a).

The small-scale garment manufacturers in particular were wary of diversifying into women's wear. The quotas for women's garments were relatively more expensive to buy, and the conversion costs were higher due to the complexity in manufacturing women's garments. Rapidly changing fashion trends in women's wear was an additional deterrent for the small-scale manufacturing units, as this meant constant research and adaptation to survive in this market, and they were thus hesitant to produce women's wear in large volumes.[12] Technical difficulties were another obstacle; women's clothing required several embellishments, such as buttons, threads, and lining. The raw materials had to be imported, and that drove up the cost of production. This made it difficult, especially for the small-scale producers, to offer competitive prices.

Diversifying into baby wear presented even more acute problems. Interviewees indicated that infant wear often required embellishments such as the cartoon character Winnie the Pooh, and care had to be taken to avoid irritants to delicate baby skin. In general, the more the work required on a product, the less the production.[13] It seems that Pakistani garment manufacturers were hesitant to venture into niche markets and preferred to manufacture men's garments because profits were stable and the work was less complex, even if they had to forgo higher profit margins.[14]

In the same vein, knitwear in general and cotton knitted shirts for men and boys in particular also have the advantage of a relatively short and simpler back process of production compared with the woven sector. The back process in the knitwear subsector consists of spinning cotton into yarn, knitting yarn into grey fabrics, dyeing, printing and fabrication, and stitching of the garment. The most important stage in this process is fabrication. Pakistani manufacturers were able to acquire the inputs, the machinery and technology, needed to manufacture garments that suited various foreign buyers. In contrast, the back process in the woven sector is longer, more tedious, and involves more capital and resources. The weaving plants require sophisticated machinery and technology, and thus, more start-up capital. It is also important to note that in competitor countries such as Bangladesh, the exporters were free to import fabrics from any part of the world and then export after adding value, due to incentives such as the 12 percent duty exemption in EU countries enjoyed by Bangladesh under the GSP. In Pakistan, the import of woven fabrics was initially not permitted by ROO (refer to chapter 5, endnote 23) and was also protected by tariff. For export purposes, there existed a number of temporary import schemes that allowed duty-free import of fabrics and other inputs. However, this was made complicated by a wide array of compliance requirements. Due to the limited access to inputs, the industry started relying more on producing knitwear and was unable to diversify toward woven garments. For new entrepreneurs, it was relatively easier and more manageable to establish knitwear plants and produce knitted shirts for men.

One of the key issues explored in the interviews was the factors explaining the success of individual exporters and the success of the RMG sector as a whole. More specifically, the research question was whether the success was a result of entrepreneurial efforts undertaken by individual garment manufacturers and exporters or a result of government support or other processes including various forms of linkages.

Not surprisingly, most garment manufacturers responded by highlighting various aspects of their own entrepreneurship and efforts and singled out their own hard work as the reason for their success. For example, Mr. Asif Tata, Managing Director of Naveena Exporters, identified two key reasons that enabled his firm to be among the top five garment manufacturers in Pakistan: first, consistent teamwork and coordination among his staff and, second, the realization that "each foreign buyer is different" and the ability to understand what the buyers are looking for and follow their requirement closely. He said that because of his team's initiative, hard work, and research, Naveena Exporters continued to be a strong competitor even after the phaseout of the quota system. Sana Merchant, speaking on behalf of S. M. Traders and S. M. Garments, agreed, and stated that it was the hard work and experience of her grandfather, who originally started this family-owned business, that had brought the companies consistent success in recent years. She explained that because S. M. Traders was a family-owned business, "it was our in-house man power and the fact that we've been in the business for very long, and thus our experience, that have made us successful exporters." Ghulam Mohammed, the Managing Director of Globe Managements (Pvt.) Ltd., stated, "It was simply our entrepreneurial effort," and Adnan Hameed from Union Garments agreed, observing that "our firm commitments, good workmanship, and our hardworking staff were the key to our success." But he added, "I am sorry to say, none of the governments introduced any good policy to help out the garments industry." Therefore, almost all the garment manufacturers interviewed highlighted their own individual efforts as accounting for their success and did not feel that any particular policies of the Government of Pakistan had helped them.

When reflecting on the sector as a whole, manufacturers were reluctant to categorize it as a success story. But buying agents like Ms. Ulrike Agnes, head of the buying service Texflow, which connects European buyers with the local textile industries in Pakistan, optimistically noted, "I do think it's a success story, because you know 30–40 years ago we did not even have a garment industry. I think the quotas played a big role. They ensured that we got a piece of the pie." However, Asif Merchant of S. M. Traders highlighted "low productivity, inefficiency, and wastage issues" as the reasons why the Pakistani garment industry had not realized its full potential and was still far behind competitors like Bangladesh and India. Ghulam Mohammed of Globe Managements categorically stated that "there was not an industry back then and there is none at the moment. Compare our situation with all of our competitors. I think it's a failure, because we should be far ahead."[15] The subjective opinions of manufacturers are valuable, but may not accord with economic reality. In Table 6.2 we note the sector's performance at the turn of the century.[16]

Table 6.2 Export growth, value, and export share of the Pakistani RMG sector

Growth period	Percentage growth	Fiscal year	Value (mil. $s)	RMG as a % of total exports
2004–2005 to 2005–2006	31.0	2005–2006	10,002.0	8.3
2003–2004 to 2004–2005	2.9	2004–2005	765.1	8.2
2002–2003 to 2003–2004	−7.5	2003–2004	891.2	10.1
2001–2002 to 2002–2003	24.2	2002–2003	880.2	9.7
2000–2001 to 2001–2002	6.4	2001–2002	708.9	9.9

The figures for 2004–2005 and 2005–2006 are provisional and growth computations are based on nominal dollars. For importer country data that are essentially consistent with Table 6.2, refer to Table 2.2 and Annex 2, Table A and B.
Source: Government of Pakistan, *Economic Surveys*, (2001–2002, p. 117; 2002–2003, p. 130; 2003–2004, p. 101; 2004–2005, p. 116; 2005–2006, p. 128).

Table 6.2 shows that growth has fluctuated, but that the RMG export share has been sizable and steady. While abolition of quotas has presented the buyers with an option to source from the most efficient and cost-effective vendors and countries, it has also opened a Pandora's box for the suppliers: stiff global competition driven by low costs and new legislation in high-income countries. Thus the RMG sector in Pakistan is in a very precarious position, and it remains to be seen how it meets the post-MFA challenge. Although Table 6.2 shows a pickup in growth in the first year post-MFA period, some signs, as earlier noted, are not favorable.

6.4. Role of the Government: Hindrance or Help?

Questions on government policy elicited a range of responses, with very few manufacturers acknowledging that the government had indeed introduced several helpful schemes to boost the garments sector. Most manufacturers believed that in principle the government's role was vital for the survival of the sector in the post-MFA era; however, in light of the lack of significant results, many viewed its interventions as more of a nuisance than help and preferred that "interference" by the government be restricted to a minimum.

The main issue that was highlighted by many of the large-scale garment manufacturers was the difficulty in attracting foreign buyers and their businesses to Pakistan in the midst of security and political concerns. The first factor that a potential buyer considers about a supplier country is whether the country has a stable political climate in terms of government and trade policies. Political stability and security for trade was one area where many manufacturers felt that the Pakistani government should be playing an active role, because it was crucial to the survival of the garment industry in the country.

Perhaps none explained this better than Mr. Asif Tata from Naveena Exporters when he said, "Half of my battle is won when I get my buyers to land in Karachi." This statement rang true with many other manufacturers as well. Sana Merchant, speaking on behalf of S. M. Traders, stated, "We have never had a foreign company come to Pakistan and check out our factory or our goods. Usually we go abroad to sell our garments." Other exporters agreed, saying that their top management officials travel to the United States and Europe around eight to ten times a year.

The government officials interviewed highlighted the key measures that the government has undertaken with regards to supporting the textile industry and stated that they had clear goals, based on the Textile Vision of Pakistan 2005, to cope with the post-MFA scenario. The central issue explored in this context was the government's role in bettering the image of Pakistan in global investment circles to encourage foreign buyers to do business with Pakistani manufacturers. Further, they recognized the responsibility of the government in the crucial tasks of promoting research and development (R&D), supporting local production of textile machinery, establishing institutes to impart the necessary training and education, setting up the infrastructure that the sector needs, supporting and establishing standards for contamination free cotton,[17] and providing incentives and subsidies as called for and permissible under the WTO trade rules.[18] A high-level Federal Textile Board has been established with the Textile Commissioner's Office serving as the secretariat. While government officials recognized the negative impact of security concerns, they also indicated that until ground realities changed and the security situation improved, exporters could not count on much progress in this regard.

Thus, Pakistan, notwithstanding its close alliance with the United States in the "war on terror," is still on the travel advisory list of the U.S. State Department, and as a consequence, big brand name companies avoid sending their employees to Pakistan. Also, the war on terror has resulted in visa restrictions, and the middle management of Pakistani companies could not go as easily to Europe and United States, even though that is the only option they have to make a sales pitch.[19] To defray this additional expense, garment exporters have suggested that the government provide 5 percent of total travel cost as a subsidy.[20]

Representatives of the Trade Development Authority of Pakistan (TDAP) stated that the government was aware of this issue and that support for travel was likely to be forthcoming.[21] They also mentioned that in response to widespread demand, the government had provided a 6 percent (of total cost) R&D subsidy to garment manufacturers on exports of woven and knitted garments, on the basis of FOB value, since fiscal 2004–2005. However, most manufacturers viewed this subsidy as a feeble attempt by the government to provide some temporary support in the wake of the quota phaseout rather than as a measure of sustained support for R&D in the RMG sector.[22]

Manufacturers also suggested that the government contribute to the training and skills of the workers. All of the interviewed manufacturers and buying agents argued that no matter how efficient and time-saving the machines are, the garment sector is labor-intensive and investment in skills is what will make Pakistan competitive. The required machines and technology can be acquired, but its proper utilization by a skilled and educated workforce is also crucial. Government officials pointed out that the government had given the initial funding for various institutes such as the notable

Pakistan Readymade Garments Technical Training Institute (PRGTTI) in Karachi that opened in 1997 to train workers and offers courses on various industry-related topics like merchandizing and garment machine mechanics.[23]

Even so, manufacturers pointed to constraints limiting the effectiveness of institutes like the PRGTTI. Workers in the small-scale industries who were illiterate and semi-skilled, and required training the most, could not take advantage of this opportunity, because they could not afford the fees or take time out for training. Similarly, factory managers and supervisors could not leave their workplace to attend training sessions. Thus, manufacturers called for on-the-job training support on issues like managing the production line, particularly for the small-scale enterprises.

In response, the government started a Sewing Operators Training Program (SOTP) in the late 1990s, which imparts on-site training to workers. This is a three-month course, and during the training the government pays 50 percent of the stipend and the factory owner the other 50 percent. At the culmination of the training, the workers are employed in the same factory. While this scheme was lauded for achieving its desired objective, manufacturers suggested that more schemes of this nature needed to be implemented if the small-scale garment sector workforce was to succeed in the future.

The Textile Garments Skill Development Board was set up in the Ministry of Textile Industry in pursuance of the 2005–2006 policy initiative for supporting the textile and garment sector. As part of the board's initiatives, garment manufacturing units were to be developed as skill development training institutes.[24] The board, comprising prominent bureaucrats from the Ministry of Commerce and the Ministry of Textile Industry, and noted officials from the TDAP and major garment manufacturing associations, such as the Pakistan Readymade Garment Export Association (PRGMEA), initiated the training program in mid-2006 to train a critical mass of 20,000 to 22,500 workers in one year, at Karachi, Lahore and Faisalabad.[25] The government contributed Rs. 2,500 per month per trainee as stipend and Rs. 1,000 per month toward the fee of the trainer.[26]

The 44 manufacturing units that agreed to participate planned to train 15 to 40 candidates each and allocate all workers individual machines for the training. A welcome feature of this scheme was that female workers, who met the eligibility requirements, had 75 percent of the seats in each unit reserved for them. The scheme was designed for new trainees, and those already working as machine operators were not eligible. Government of Pakistan (2007, p. 38) reported that 30 units continued with the program and enrolled candidates in consecutive batches up to a total of

10,000–12,000 trainees per year, and that the scope of the program is to be broadened to include the terry towel and bed linen subsectors.

The Government of Pakistan has also launched a Stitching Machine Operator Training Program (SMOT) in which selected garment factories are declared as training institutions. In the first phase of the program, launched in June 2006, 555 candidates were trained in 18 garment units. This scheme plans to train 6,000 stitching machine operators for the garment sector. A total of 3,729 persons have been trained under the SMOT since 2006. Out of these trained persons, 3,152 were employed in garment units during 2006–2007.

The government has declared its intentions to fully support the shift toward value-added goods. It has launched a Pakistan Textile City Project and has also established three "garment cities," one each in Karachi, Lahore, and Faisalabad. Under the 2003 trade policy, it was envisaged that these three garment cities would be established to develop state-of-the-art facilities for garment manufacturers. The Pakistan Textile City Corporation was established and listed with the Pakistan Securities and Exchange Commission. In order to expedite the garment cities project, it was decided that it would be run as a private-public partnership and that the board of directors of each garment city company would include representatives of the private sector. All the privileges of an Export Processing Zone (EPZ) were to be extended to these cities with an assurance of quality infrastructure and utilities.

The garment cities would comprise clusters of sewing and stitching units grouped together to produce specialized garments for export and provide an opportunity to small- and medium-sized entrepreneurs to develop value-added clothing and accessories. The concept of garment cities is a departure from the vertically integrated supply chain to more fragmented and horizontal manufacturing structures required for fast-changing fashions and designer lines. The idea is to promote specialization and volumes even in small and medium enterprises, and hence enable them to realize economies of scale and enhance productivity via mutual linkages and competition. The marketing process is facilitated by buying houses and importers' agents, who can direct the production and procurement of large export products from one place. The government view is that garment cities would give a new lease on life to garment exports and attract enterprises that are not bogged down by their vertically integrated production and management systems.[27]

The Lahore Garment City Company was incorporated in September 2004 and has acquired 19.4 acres in the Sunder Industrial Estate. Seven hundred acres have been acquired for the Karachi Garment City at Port

Table 6.3 Comparative cost structure in apparel production in selected countries (2001–2002) (percentages)

Costs	Pakistan	Bangladesh	India	China
Materials	56.1	75.4	47.8	74.8
Electricity	3.5	0.7	0.9	0.0
Other energy	0.9	0.5	0.9	2.9
Wages	13.9	11.6	11.3	13.7
Benefits	0.4	2.0	0.8	0.0
Sales & general admin.	7.2	2.0	2.3	0.0
Transport/communication	3.7	0.9	28.4	1.0
Other costs	1.1	2.3	3.6	5.1
Interest and rent	13.1	4.6	4.0	2.6
Total	100.0	100.0	100.0	100.0
Cash costs as share of sales	54.1	87.1	84.0	82.8

Source: World Bank/SMEDA (2003).

Qasim, and the government has committed 45 percent of the Rs. 1.1 billion equity. Work on the Faisalabad Garment City is also progressing.[28]

When asked about what additional measures and initiatives the Government of Pakistan could take to assist the garment sector, almost all manufacturers responded with demands of cheap fuel and proper infrastructure, transportation, and access to electricity, gas, and water to assist in the production process. These are viewed as severe constraints that hinder timely production and add to the cost of production. The World Bank Investment Climate Assessment surveys provide international comparisons of cost structures that give some perspective on this issue. Table 6.3 provides an indication of the cost structure of the apparel industries in Pakistan relative to that in competitor countries.

Electricity costs, though not a large part of total costs, were still five times higher in Pakistan than in Bangladesh and almost four times than in India.[29] Similarly, transportation costs were indeed higher than those in Bangladesh and China, although considerably below those in India. However, it appears that the cost of borrowing and rental might be a constraint, even though manufacturers did not raise these issues. Businesses also need to look to containing their own sales and administrative costs, which are three times higher than those in India and Bangladesh.[30]

The businesses noted the government subsidies provided to the industry in competitor countries. For example, they mentioned a 15 percent cash subsidy on locally manufactured fabric in Bangladesh, but unlike Pakistan, the latter grows no cotton and is understandably trying to cut fabric import costs. The Chinese government apparently provides electricity completely free of charge, and Table 6.3 seems to verify this.

Industrialists also made self-serving suggestions, including that yarn and fabric should not be given preferential treatment (such as the 3 percent subsidy given by the government to fabric exporters in the trade year 2006–2007 and that cotton exports should be banned. While an economic case can be made for not providing more favorable treatment to yarn or grey cloth exports, there is little economic justification for a ban on cotton export to provide cotton to the domestic textile industry at below world market prices. Lower raw material transportation cost in any case provides an edge, and this accounts for the lower material cost for Pakistan relative to Bangladesh in Table 6.3.

In March 2006, the Federal Textile Minister, Mushtaq Ali Cheema, announced that a committee had been constituted at the direction of the Prime Minister to formulate recommendations for the support of the industry after MFA abolition. In July 2005, the sales tax on textile raw material had already been abolished for export-oriented industries. It was also announced that land would be provided at affordable prices to knitwear industries in the textile and garment city projects along with other reliable infrastructure facilities. The TDAP had been urged to explore new markets for the knitwear subsector, particularly among the ASEAN (Association of South East Asian Nations) and OIC (Organization of Islamic Countries) nations and in China, Japan, and South Korea. The TDAP Chairman, Mr. Tariq Ikram, said that warehousing facilities would be provided in Karachi on nominal charges, and for that purpose 20 acres had been set aside by the Sindh provincial government.

The TDAP is providing consultancy support for technology enhancement. Sales tax on export-related domestic and imported products has been zero-rated. The trade policy that was announced mentioned support for the export sector through technology upgrading, brand development, and brand marketing of Pakistan's products abroad.[31] Thus, the government appears to be attempting to assist the knitwear subsector, which has been under immense pressure after the phaseout of the MFA quota regime. The real issue naturally is policy implementation.

6.5. Other Current and Emerging Issues in the RMG Sector

6.5.1. Intrasector Relations

We explored the extent of integration and coordination among the RMG companies with a focus on collective action to face challenges. Such networking and joint action is facilitated by and reinforces social capital in this industrial context (refer to section 1.4). From the interviews conducted and the information gleaned, it appeared that most garment manufacturers and exporters are connected through various organizations such as the PRGMEA and the PKSEA.

Our interviewees explained that all the garment companies communicated with each other and stayed abreast of the news and information relating to the sector. The level of joint action and collaboration was particularly high when the sector was faced with a crisis, such as a shortage of yarn or the advent of a new tax levied on the manufacturers. When the quotas were phased out, the sector developed a joint strategy of pushing for the 6 percent R&D subsidy and succeeded in getting it. To contend with a crisis, joint meetings are held within the association and representations taken to the government to seek further assistance.

6.5.2. The Process of Technology Diffusion

Most of the large-scale manufacturers we interviewed had imported machinery and had locally obtained a few ancillary and subsidiary parts. For example, the knitted garment manufacturers in particular imported the machinery needed in their fabrication units from Japan and Korea. The dyeing and printing units and denim plants were all established as a result of an import-friendly policy. This was also the case with integrated units embodying the whole value chain. The government enabled duty-free import of machinery based on selling three-year indemnity bonds and many manufacturers took advantage of this facility.[32] One manufacturer indicated that "most of the entrepreneurs traveled to similar factories abroad and brought back their ideas [those of the factories abroad] and the relevant technology with them." Foreign buyers also gave leads to the garment exporters about particular software and machinery that produced the best results. Sometimes, technology transfer resulted from a joint venture.

However, it appears that only the large-scale industries, with more than 3,000 employees, imported machinery. As indicated earlier, the garment sector in Pakistan is extremely fragmented with small-scale units accounting for 88 percent of the total. The cutting and sewing capacities in these units are substandard because the machinery is often out-of-date and since it is poorly maintained and adjusted as the mechanics lack training. This prevents the small-scale units from meeting the required international quality standards. Details of the age of the capital stock are provided in Table 6.4 in a comparative context.

Table 6.4 The age distribution and median age of capital stock in Pakistan and Bangladesh in the RMG sector (percentages)

Age of capital stock	Pakistan	Bangladesh
<5 years	14	47
5–10 years	28	40
10–20 years	35	13
>20 years	23	0
Total	100	100
Median years	12	5

Source: World Bank (2004).

Table 6.4 indicates that the capital equipment in the RMG sector in Pakistan is much older than in Bangladesh. The median age of capital equipment is twelve years in Pakistan compared with five years in Bangladesh. The equipment is older in Pakistan naturally because of the head start it got in this sector. Given the very rapid development of technology in this sector, the old installed capital equipment at the plant level is an opportunity, since it provides greater scope for raising productivity by modernizing the capital stock. However, raising the required funds for such modernization is a challenge for the small-scale sector. According to Government of Pakistan (2007, p. 37), Pakistani businesses spent about $6 billion on machinery upgrades, mostly in spinning and weaving, between 1999 and 2006 in preparation for the MFA phaseout.

6.5.3. Challenges

After the MFA phaseout, Pakistan is confronting intense competition from many countries. Businesses pointed out that Bangladesh had privileged access to EU markets (refer to chapter 3), and China and India, with their ability to realize economies of scale, also are challenging competitors.[33] The Sub-Saharan African countries, Sri Lanka, Jordan, and Mexico enjoy free trade agreements with the United States and thus get preferred access to the market. Turkey has easier access to the EU market, and its units are relocating to Egypt, which has much to gain from the greater efficiency of Turkish companies, for privileged access to the U.S. market.

While the WTO rules out direct subsidies, Pakistani manufacturers claim that various cash subsidies and input subsidies are being provided to producers in Bangladesh, China, and India.[34] In any case, Pakistani manufacturers will need to improve efficiency and reduce wastage. This is important in the postquota world because the rewards of success are much greater and, by the same token, the costs of failure are also much greater. Elbehri, Hertel, and Martin (2003) concluded in a study of the garment sector in India that the benefits of increasing productivity in the textile sector had more than doubled after abolition of the quotas, primarily because of the increase in the price responsiveness of the demand for textile and clothing exports. Prior to quota abolition, exporters faced totally price-inelastic demand in the major world markets.

A World Bank-SMEDA (2003) study concluded that, on average, customs clearance took 17 days in Pakistan compared with seven in China and 12 in Bangladesh. While there is considerable controversy about the validity of this specific number, interviews with industry participants reveal concerns about the efficiency of customs processes and related procedures for rebating and exempting duties on inputs under the Duty and Tax Rebate for Exporters (DTRE) scheme. Higher clearance times, in particular, can prove costly for garment producers relying on international sourcing for their intermediate inputs. This is because such delays force them to hold higher inventories, but more importantly because delays increase their response time to new orders and expose them to the consequent risk of losing these orders and future ones.[35]

Complying with standards pertaining to health and safety, and more recently the environment, built into the "code of conduct" of the buyers, is another challenge, particularly for small-scale garment manufacturing units. Several of the small-scale units have been found to have violated these standards, negatively impacting exports. The government could step in here and help small-scale units meet international standards.

6.5.4. Partnerships and Close Relationships with Foreign Firms

Several of the large-scale garment companies in Pakistan maintained close contact with their foreign buyers and collaborated with them on key areas, as the examples that follow will illustrate. Mr. Asif Riaz Tata referred to a "strategic partnership" of Naveena Exporters with Target, a U.S. retail store. This partnership ensured that the two companies were in touch regularly, and Target bought a specified number of garments according to a predetermined schedule. Employees of Naveena Exporters were provided access to the Target Web site and could update the progress on orders and delivery online. In addition, Target had also assisted in training the management and employees at Naveena and conducted regular seminars to teach them how to update information on the Target Web site. Mr. Tata termed the training useful and said that "with them (Target) we are continuously enhancing our skills and our management systems." Mr. Aziz Memon,

Chairman of Kings Apparel, one of the most successful garment companies in Pakistan, indicated that his company maintained a close relationship with the U.S. retail giant Wal-Mart. This involved preset orders and collaboration on quality and compliance issues to make sure both parties understood each other perfectly. Mr. Ghulam Mohammed informed us that his company, Globe Managements, worked with ten major customers and had been supplying big brands such as Wrangler and Liz Claiborne for many years. In particular, they enjoyed a close relationship with Wrangler with regard to sharing of knowledge and training and held a joint conference every three to six months to discuss goals and targets.

Prior to 2005, buyer strategies were governed by the availability of quotas rather than supplier efficiency. Quota abolition has provided an opportunity to the buyers to select efficient and cost-competitive suppliers. They are developing mutually beneficial, long-term relationships with their key suppliers. While suppliers anticipate a constant flow of orders, buyers induce operational efficiencies in their supply chain through reduced times in product development cycles, standardization of processes, logistics routing, and inventory visibility. In addition, there has also been a shift from fragmented sourcing to full-package suppliers who have capabilities from design to development. This helps suppliers reduce the lead time for their products and also shrinks concept-to-store timelines.[36]

These changes have become evident in Pakistan in the past two years. Mr. Atiq Kochra, drawing on his experience of the garment sector as a manufacturer and a buying agent, explained that there had been several cases of foreign buyers investing in Pakistan or engaging in a joint venture with a Pakistani company. He mentioned a few recent cases of Italian businessmen setting up a high-end vertical unit for knitwear in Karachi's Korangi Industrial area and also a few projects that had materialized in the province of Punjab. Gulf Exports of Bahrain has collaborated with Nishat Mills to establish a garment factory in Lahore. Several buying agents in Pakistan are also helping their foreign buyers forge ties with the local small-scale industries. It is still early to assess the macro export significance of such partnerships.

6.5.5. Future of the RMG Sector: Prospects and Predictions

Pakistan was stated to be among the initial losers from the MFA phaseout; its exports to the U.S. and EU markets declined by 0.8 percent in 2005.[37] Initial estimates from PRGMEA indicate that about 150 out of about 2, 500 units in Karachi have shut down after MFA abolition.[38] The knitted garments subsector was particularly in a bad shape because the small-scale knitwear units were no longer able to compete. The larger suppliers of knitted garments, who had invested in developing their capabilities in manufacturing, product development, and design, continued to do well. These companies successfully moved away from solely price-based competition to providing long-term strategic partnerships and higher value-added services to their buyers.

The woven garment sector in Pakistan also continued to perform well. It had been a consistent performer during the quota regime, with men's/boys' cotton trousers constituting 16.67 percent of exports in 2003.[39] In the quota-free era, it continues to enjoy advantages. Pakistani cotton has a short staple fiber length and the spinning sector in the country is geared toward weaving this into very good quality coarse yarn. This comparative advantage has enabled Pakistan to gradually become a good supplier of woven garments, which are manufactured from these coarser fabrics. As a result, in terms of exports, Pakistan is doing particularly well in the product categories of "bottoms," such as men's trousers, pants, denim jeans, and shorts, and this specialization is a possible future trend.

Summary and Conclusion

Our key research question is about understanding the processes, including various kinds of linkages, accounting for successful garment exports. For Pakistan, it appears that this can be accounted for by the dynamic of success breeding success in the case of export of men's and boys' shirts. The initial high quota allocation for this product, because of high local cotton production, started the process. The internal dynamic was that high exports resulted in higher export quotas, and so those that started doing well continued to do well. Industrial policy helped at this stage with a number of incentives.

Curiously, garment exporters stuck with men's and boys' shirts and did not diversify. It appears that they followed the path of least resistance. Even though the margins were likely to be higher, they avoided baby wear and women's wear because of the greater risk and complexity associated with these products.

After the MFA phaseout on January 1, 2005, Pakistan had already started losing market share even in men's and boys' shirts to India, which overtook Pakistan in value terms for this product category in the first year after the quotas were removed. Overall, the growth of Pakistan's exports to the EU and U.S. markets has been sustained, but it is nowhere near that recorded by China and India.

The government has undertaken several schemes to help the industry cope with the greater competition post-MFA, but only a few industrialists thought that enough is being done or that what is being done is effective.

As government assistance is crucial to their success, they are demanding more schemes and speedier implementation of them. The government for now is not responding to further industry demands and is looking for greater competitive effort from within the industry.

There was evidence of joint action within the garment sector and the industry more broadly, particularly when the industry faced a crisis such as the quota phaseout. Much of this takes the form of collectively lobbying the government for support or concessions.

Notwithstanding the extensive industrial policy incentives, training, and R&D support, Pakistani garment manufacturers and exporters viewed their pre-MFA success to be mostly a result of their own efforts. They cited their efforts at obtaining the necessary technology and their striving for common goals through various trade associations and partnerships with foreign firms. This, in their view, assisted in cementing Pakistan's position as one of the leading garment manufacturing countries in the world.

However, in the wake of the phaseout of the quota system, Pakistan finds itself competing for its share in the global garment market, as it strives for changes in product competencies at home. It appears that the next decade of RMG exports in Pakistan may be dominated by woven wear, in particular trousers and pants for men and boys, since the kind and quality of cotton grown in Pakistan provides a competitive advantage for this product. Pakistan can serve this niche by presenting itself as a competitive and reliable supplier for "bottoms" via the necessary investments. Garment manufacturers and exporters will need to provide a complete value-added package, including innovation, design, quality, service, and speedy and reliable delivery to their buyers. Government industrial policy will need to facilitate this process, as it did in the initial stages, to reinforce the success of the textile industry in general and the garment sector in particular.

Annexure 6.1

List of Interviewees in Pakistan

Mr. Asif Riaz Tata, Chairman, Naveena Exporters (Pvt.) Ltd., Karachi, and former Chairman of Pakistan Knitwear & Sweaters Exporters Association.

Mr. Aziz Memon, Chairman, Kings Apparel, Karachi, and Chairman of Karachi Garment City Company Limited.

Mr. Nusrat Jamshed, Executive Director of Textiles, Export Promotion Bureau of Pakistan, Karachi.

Mr. Amir Jan, Director, Export Promotion Bureau of Pakistan, Karachi.

Mr. Asad Zahoor, Executive Director, Supply Chain Development Export Promotion Bureau of Pakistan, Karachi.

Mr. Asif Merchant, Managing Director of Garments, S. M. Traders Pvt. Ltd., Karachi.

Ms. Sana Merchant, Managing Director of Garments, S. M. Traders Pvt. Ltd., Karachi.

Mr. Adnan Hameed, Managing Director of Apparel/Garments, Union Garments, Lahore.

Mr. Nadeem Ahmed, Managing Director, Texlink Buying Services, Karachi.

Mr. Ghulam Mohammed, Managing Director of Garments, Globe Managements Pvt. Ltd., Karachi.

Mr. Atiq A. Kochra, Managing Director, Rubytex Sourcing, Karachi, and former Zonal Chairman, Pakistan Readymade Garments Manufacturers & Exporters Association (PRGMEA).

Dr. Arif Patel, Sales/Production of Garments, Al-Munaf Corporation, Karachi.

Mrs. Ulrike Agne Qureshi, Managing Director, Texflow Buying Services, Karachi.

Mr. Javed Akhtar, President, Akhtar Textiles Pvt. Ltd., Karachi.

Ms. Abida Ahmed, Dawood Lawrencepur Ltd., Karachi.

CHAPTER 7

The Readymade Garments Sector in Sri Lanka

7.1. Introduction

As in the other South Asian countries we studied, in Sri Lanka too, the textile and garment industry has played, and continues to play, a significant role in the economy. Kelegama (2005, pp. 51–53) reported that by the 1990s, garments had replaced tea as the country's highest foreign exchange earner. By 2002, textiles and garments, predominantly the latter, accounted for "6 percent of GDP, 39 percent of industrial production, 33 percent of manufacturing employment,[1] 52 percent of total exports, and 67 percent of industrial exports." As is the case with other South Asian economies, with the phasing out of the MFA on January 1, 2005, the Sri Lankan economy, highly reliant on RMG exports, has become vulnerable to the changing global circumstances affecting the RMG sector. In such a trade milieu, strengthening the competitiveness of the garment sector and addressing various constraints have become critical, and we address this issue in this chapter.

In section 2, we briefly review the history of the textile and garment industry. In section 3, we explore the causes of the RMG sector's export success and review the current state of affairs, based on interviews with senior management of firms in this sector. In section 4, we review the lost opportunities and measures that can help build an integrated textile industry supporting a thriving garment sector.

7.2. History of the Textile and Garment Industry in Sri Lanka

As early as the 1950s, three private companies, Hentley Shirts (Pvt.) Ltd., Dia Shirts Company, and Maxim Shirts (Pvt.) Ltd., manufactured men's shirts for the Sri Lankan market.[2] In the early half of the 1960s, Hentley

Shirts exported a few consignments of shirts to countries in East Asia; but this trade was not conducted on a large scale or in an organized manner and did not lead to an evolution of marketing strategies. However, in the late 1960s, Gil Garments (Pvt.) Ltd. ventured into international markets on a large scale with the production of denim jeans for both men and women.[3]

Between 1970 and 1977, Sirimavo Bandaranayake's government envisioned a self-sufficient Sri Lanka and formulated a national economic policy to attain this goal. For this purpose, the government imposed heavy taxes and other restrictions on all imported goods and encouraged local industrialists and entrepreneurs to invest in new industries to meet national consumption needs. Simultaneously, the government urged citizens to reject imported goods to support local industries. However, due to dwindling foreign exchange reserves and import restrictions, industrialists were unable to import vital inputs (i.e., machinery, technical expertise, and raw materials). Despite an influx of financial capital during the 1970s, the lack of inputs contributed to the stagnation of most industries including the textile industry.

J. R. Jayewardene came to power in 1977, and his government was intent on speeding up economic development, particularly, to reduce the rising youth unemployment rate.[4] The government was also keen to stake a claim in the burgeoning global economy and to replenish the dwindling foreign exchange reserves. It adopted an open economic policy stance and lifted all restrictions on imports. The government encouraged local entrepreneurs and appealed to foreign businesses to set up garment factories in the newly established free-trade zones (FTZ). The incentives included subsidies, duty-rebate schemes, duty-free imports of machinery and materials, tax holidays, and lower corporation taxes.[5] As indicated earlier in this volume, protectionism in high-income countries, in the form of MFA quotas, helped Sri Lanka to develop its export-oriented garment sector by insulating it from direct competition from more established producers and by attracting quota-hoppers.

With the liberalization of the economy, the country's RMG sector gained momentum, and much of its success was due to the quota-hopping East Asian and other garment manufacturers who were attracted by Sri Lanka's liberal stance on international trade and established RMG units in the country.[6] However, contrary to the previous government's policy stance, the new administration concentrated solely on encouraging investment in the RMG sector and neglected support for the broader textile industry and auxiliary sectors (including cotton, yarn, weaving mills, dyes, buttons, and zippers) necessary for the long-term sustainability of the RMG sector. Thus, the main feature of garment factories established in Sri Lanka toward the end of the 1970s was that they were limited to the activities of cutting, sewing, and packing. Although the government boasted about foreign exchange earnings, the actual foreign exchange earnings from the RMG sector were less than 20 percent of the total foreign exchange earnings.[7] As indicated earlier, the reliance on foreign inputs limited the net foreign exchange earnings.

By early 1980s, garment exports were growing rapidly, and by 1986 garments accounted for the largest share of exports (27 percent).[8] Even so, as Kelegama pointed out (p. 52), until the late 1980s, the garment sector in Sri Lanka was referred to in the country as "glorified tailor shops," because, despite a decade of growth, its links with other industries remained underdeveloped and the sector's product value-added continued to be low.

During the 1990s, the RMG sector continued to grow at about 18.5 percent per annum. Moreover, by the end of the 1990s, the garment sector was contributing to the livelihood of nearly 1.2 million people in addition to the direct employment of about 330,000.[9] However, the boom period for the sector appeared to have come to an end with the phasing out of the MFA. Sri Lanka struggled as regional trading blocs and bilateral free-trade agreements proliferated to govern nearly 33 percent of global trade, and China and India emerged as major suppliers of garments at very competitive rates.[10]

Although Sri Lanka experienced a setback in the immediate aftermath of the MFA, a year later, as benefits of bilateral trade pacts that Sri Lanka was party to started kicking in, the RMG sector appeared to make a moderate recovery. During the 12-month period ending in February of 2006, Sri Lanka shipped US$244.9 million worth of apparel—a rise of 10 percent—with order books nearly full for the first six months of 2006.[11]

According to Kelegama (2005), about 850 garment factories now account for about half of Sri Lanka's total exports earnings. Nearly 63 percent of the garments are shipped to the United States and 30 percent to European Union; hence there is not much market diversification. Just 12 percent of the factories account for about 72 percent of the exports; hence there is a high degree of market concentration. Some of the top producers have developed strong and reliable links with well-known international retailers. Sri Lankan entrepreneurs have started to invest in the industry in a substantial way and have also opened up units in other places like Bangladesh, Maldives, Jordan, Kenya, and Mauritius for delivering on orders.[12] We turn next to the findings based on our interviews with the top management of RMG firms.[13]

7.3. Survey Findings

7.3.1. Networking, Social Capital, and Local-Foreign Partnerships

Currently, RMG manufacture accounts for nearly 93 percent of the textile/apparel industry in Sri Lanka (Kelegama 2005). The most successful garment exports from Sri Lanka are HS 6204 (women's or girls' suits and similar items under this category), HS 6203 (men's or boys' suits and similar items under this category), and HS 6206 (women's or girls' blouses and similar items under this category). Sri Lanka has also become a well-known top exporter of women's lingerie.[14] In this chapter, following the criteria described in chapter 1, our focus is on HS 620469 (women's and girl's trousers, shorts, materials, not knit).

To explore the causes of export success at the product level, senior managers of 13 readymade garment units, which had manufactured HS 620469 in substantial quantity over the last 10–12 years, were interviewed in the summer of 2006.[15] The manufacturers included large-scale units operating with a capital stock of up to Sri Lankan Rupees (SLR) 400 million and small-scale apparel units operating with a capital stock of about SLR 1 million.[16] All 13 manufacturers produced RMG exclusively for exports and all, except for two [Avro Garments (Pvt.) Ltd. and Serendib (Pvt.) Ltd.], came directly under the purview of the Board of Investment (BOI) in Sri Lanka.[17]

The interviewees could not comment on whether the demand for the product category HS620469 had been high throughout the past decade and also could not specify the exact proportion of HS620469 in total output. This is mainly because demand changes almost weekly, and exporters have to keep abreast of the changes in the fashion industry and changing buyer preferences. Thus, the factories visited were equipped to manufacture multiple products in the same production lines to minimize delays. For example, a line that produces ladies' trousers this week would most probably manufacture ladies' evening wear next week. Therefore, in most factories, production technology is geared to cater to highly volatile demand for individual products. This makes it difficult for manufacturers to comment on the manufacturing and export trends of a single commodity.

The RMG manufacturers in Sri Lanka are closely networked. Most of the professionals and technicians in the industry began their careers in the textile industry. They completed their education in the same or similar schools in Sri Lanka, pursued higher education abroad in the United Kingdom, United States, and India, and started their professional careers in state-owned textile mills in the late 1960s. These connections or networks have also been beneficial for the development of the RMG sector in Sri Lanka.[18] For example, when a company is unable to complete an order on time, it requests the use of the manufacturing capacity of another manufacturer.

Thus, it could be gleaned from the interviews that RMG manufacturers within the country assist each other immensely and look out for each other. One of the recurring themes in the interviews was that Sri Lankan RMG manufacturers generally do not compete with each other to attract foreign buyers; rather, Sri Lankan manufacturers stand together to compete with other countries (other South Asian and South East Asian countries) to attract potential buyers. The establishment of many associations for mutual cooperation has strengthened ties between the companies and enhanced the ability to compete in the world markets with RMG giants such as India and China.[19]

Cooperation tends to be confined within similar production scales for technical reasons. Thus, large-scale manufacturers tend to cooperate only with other such manufacturers who work under similar conditions, similar operating capacities, and with similar advanced technologies. These mutual relationships also ensure the meeting of quality specifications established by foreign buyers. For example, buyers often have trade agreements with a couple of different manufacturers and do not mind if the product is delivered by a similar-scale producer of good reputation. Furthermore, most of the companies interviewed saw the advantage of establishing formal partnerships with foreign buyers. The view of our respondents was that such partnerships provided extra oversight that in turn improved quality.

7.3.2. Problems Identified by Manufacturers

This section is based on interviews with the senior management of manufacturing units and represents their point of view. There was a consensus among the manufacturers (large, medium, and small-scale) on what *exactly* is required to be done by the government as well as the associations such as Joint Apparel Association Forum (JAAF) to make the RMG sector more profitable. The problems are presented category wise according to the responses of the interviewees.

A set of problems arise from the dependency on imported materials. An RMG factory requests samples of fabrics and other essential inputs from suppliers abroad after finalizing an order from an importer. A whole day is spent on getting the samples, testing the quality, and negotiating the price and other terms and conditions before finally placing the order. Foreign factories need a minimum of eight weeks to execute the order. There can be unforeseen delays in shipping the order, and also delays at the Sri Lankan harbor in clearing the merchandize. Invariably, the quality of fabrics received is not up to the specifications of the sample approved. For example, damage in the middle of a fabric roll may not be evident at first glance. Even so, the factories are not in a position to reject the order completely, as they have to finish the order before the contract date expires. The usual defects in the imported fabric include weaving defects, improper width, and shade differences across rolls. Due to the substandard material and accessories there are huge wastages and in some cases it becomes difficult to deliver on an order. Due to escalating oil prices, transportation of raw material has become extremely expensive, and this reduces the profit margins.

Our respondents claimed that profit margins are also eroded by sky-rocketing electricity prices.[20] Stringent environmental protection laws and regulations (both local laws and those imposed by the buyers' code of conduct) require manufacturers to establish their own effluent treatment plants and water softening plants, and this adds to unit costs. Manufacturers also claimed that there is an increasing shortage of workers in the industry. Social stigma and evils portrayed by the media as associated with the sector (rape, abuse, uninhabitable workplaces) discourage workers, especially rural women, from seeking employment in a garment factory.

Although sewing, cutting, and packaging processes have been streamlined in most factories, washing facilities are largely lacking (i.e., specialized washing facilities for denims and fabric effects, such as stone washing). In times of high demand, it has been extremely difficult to deliver orders on time due to the lack of laundry facilities. Commercial RMG washing facilities are extremely expensive to set up, and presently a large proportion of RMG manufacturers rely on hotel laundry facilities and a few other large-scale commercial laundries. Thus, there is a need for setting up large-scale commercial laundries to support the RMG sector.[21]

Manufacturers complained of different companies'/buyers' having different codes of conduct, making conformity a challenge.[22] Some of these codes of conduct are very stringent in the context of the conditions that prevail in the manufacturer country. For example, factories must have toilets that are equipped with bidet showers, toilet paper, and have proper ventilation, facilities that are common only in upper-class houses. Also, the manufacturer is required to hire professional cleaning services to maintain proper sanitation. The actual manufacturing facility needs to be air-conditioned, again, a luxury in Sri Lanka. The employer has to provide all meals to employees and transportation to women workers.

7.3.3. Policy Suggestions

The government needs to explore and address the hindrances to the development of the textile industry and the auxiliary industries of the

RMG sector. The policy suggestions made by businesses include streamlining of port and custom regulations to prevent delays in clearance of export consignments. Owing to the lack of a fabric and accessory base, the turn-around time for Sri Lanka's garment sector is between 90 and 150 days, whereas the ideal international lead time is around 60 days. This long turnaround time is a hindrance in staying competitive, because Eastern European countries have become major suppliers of garments to the European Union, and Mexico and the Caribbean countries have become major suppliers to the United States under preferential tariff arrangements. Moreover, this problem is of particular concern because "just-in-time" delivery has become an accepted principle and requirement in the global market.

The lack of a proper network of roads and railroads causes delays in transporting raw material to the factories and finished product to the ports. The government offers tax rebates and other incentives to attract investors to build factories in rural areas but does not provide proper road networks. It expects companies to create the necessary infrastructure themselves. Manufacturers believe that it is not profitable for companies to devote resources to develop public goods, and thus, they do not venture into undeveloped areas where labor maybe plentiful.[23]

As indicated earlier (refer to Table 1.6), 41.3 percent of managers across the board found electricity to be the worst business constraint in 2003.[24] This sentiment was echoed by the managers interviewed in the RMG sector. This energy crisis is anticipated to become particularly acute in 2009. Managers informed us that the cost of production in Sri Lanka has escalated recently due to the high cost of public utilities, such as electricity, water, and telecommunications. Thirty-eight mid-scale and small-scale RMG factories had to close down between January and April 2006 due to the very high price of electricity.

Business managers in Sri Lanka, more than those in the rest of South Asia, perceived labor skills to be a constraint, despite, or perhaps because, Sri Lanka has the highest literacy and mean education rates, and therefore management has higher expectations. Managers called for the establishment of institutions to train technical staff and managers to make production more efficient and to lower unit costs.[25]

In the first half of the 1990s, a concerted effort was made to promote backward linkages with the textile industry. Government-appointed delegations were sent overseas to attract large textile producers to Sri Lanka. A number of government textile units had been established before 1977 during the import-substitution regime. They found it difficult to survive in the liberalized economy and were privatized in the early 1990s. However, subsequently, the textile industry virtually collapsed. Textile mills that had previously been shut down are being reopened in special export promotion zones. In 2005, large textile mills were built in Sri Lanka by Pakistani firms, to the concern of the All Pakistan Textile Mills Association (APTMA). The Sri Lankan government had launched a package to attract investment into the country including a ten-year tax-free period on income for investments over US$10 million. The main motivation for Pakistani businesses was getting around the ROO clause in the duty-free GSP extended to Sri Lanka by the European Union. Under the ROO clause, the RMG sector has to use fabric manufactured within the country to qualify for duty-free exports to the European Union.[26] Interestingly, restrictive trade policy in the North, similar to the MFA, is once again encouraging industrialization in the South, in this case, backward linkages.

Certain regions of Sri Lanka are conducive to the cultivation of cotton. Incentives (loans, land, machinery, improved irrigation) and technical know-how for small-scale farmers in the cotton-growing areas could help initiate cotton cultivation on a commercial scale. Textile manufacturers could also invest in cotton plantations and help produce a larger percentage of the local cotton requirements domestically. State agriculture departments and other research organizations could be encouraged to develop better quality strains of cotton with higher-yielding seeds. With an increase in the local production of cotton, ginning plants could be established in close proximity to the cotton plantations. Finally, Sri Lankan missions abroad need to help market the country's products and also help in negotiating contracts advantageous to it.

These suggestions are consistent with industrial policy support for various industries adopted by East Asian economies in their formative industrial periods. For example, Wade (2004, pp. 79–80) gives an account of state-led support for the textile industry in Taiwan in the 1950s. The next section explores the opportunities the government of Sri Lanka has missed with regard to industrial policy.

7.4. An Account of Government Failure

This section is an account of government failure as an act of omission in the "neo-developmentalist" sense of successful industrial policy, rather than as an act of commission in the neoliberal sense of too much government.[27] During the late 1960s and early 1970s, cotton production in Sri Lanka increased rapidly. The climate in the deep South was favorable for the abundant growth of cotton, and the quality of Sri Lankan cotton was far superior to the cotton that was available on the international market.

However, the cotton plantations were abandoned with the closing down of textile plants in the late 1970s.[28]

The story with regard to the loss in textile capacity is a similar lost opportunity. The main raw material requirement for the garment industry is textiles. In the late 1960s, Sri Lanka had a burgeoning textile industry with a large production capacity. The government-owned textile mills, together with a large number of privately owned textile mills, manufactured a sizable proportion of the local textile requirements. Sri Lanka also had highly qualified and technically competent personnel managing these large-scale textile plants.

As indicated earlier, the closed-economy phase in the early years of the 1970s also prohibited import of machinery and expertise from abroad. While the East Asian economies used tariff policy selectively during the import-substitution phase to develop local industry, an opportunity to learn from other countries and develop the textile industry by importing the requisite machinery, technology, and technical skills was lost because of the blanket closed-economy stance. Thus, from the late 1960s to the 1970s, there was virtually no progress in textile manufacturing.

With the change of government in 1977, and the liberalization of the economy, there was massive investment in the RMG sector, but the textile industry as a whole was completely disregarded.[29] It would have been prudent to have simultaneously developed the textile industry, based on the principal of dynamic comparative advantage, which would have given a boost to the burgeoning RMG sector. The neodevelopment policy alternatives that the government could have implemented, and those that are still relevant, were essentially the policy measures adopted by the East and South East Asian economies in the early stage of their industrial expansion, when labor-intensive industries like textiles were being encouraged.[30]

Thus, tax and other incentives (loans, interest free credit) could have been provided to existing and new textile plants to increase their capacities and productivity on the basis of measures of "success" understood and accepted by industrialists. These could include quality, profitability, or the ability of breaking into exports markets. State-of-the-art technology and machinery could have been introduced through exhibitions and technology fairs.

Training of technical personnel, at all levels, is viewed as a legitimate public sector activity, given that the private sector is unlikely to internalize the benefits due to labor mobility, and hence would not provide for this. Thus, the public sector could establish more technical schools, introduce new degree programs at universities, and sponsor training and graduate programs abroad for senior management, junior management, and other employees. Like training, due to externalities, establishing strict quality standards and setting up an accreditation institute for conformity assessment, on the basis of international practices and regulations, is not something the private sector would engage in, and hence the state should undertake this task. Partnerships with foreign investors could be selectively encouraged and incentives provided on the basis of expected benefits to the development of the garment sector, the textile industry as a whole, and the ancillary units that are a part of the industry, such as makers of dyes and chemicals. Finally, other related industries that the garment industry depends on, such as manufacturers of buttons, zip fasteners, coat hangers, and labels, need to be encouraged, while ensuring that they meet international standards. Efforts should also be made for development of designing and printing capacity for unique products of the RMG sector. Such a strategy would maximize employment and growth potential and enable moving up and internalizing the value chain. Currently, the value-added contribution of the RMG sector is estimated to vary between 20 and 30 percent (Kelegama 2005).

Finally, the codes of conduct, in terms of maintaining social and environmental standards, need to be taken seriously. While their implementation adds to the cost of production, they provide much social benefits to the country in terms of better heath and productivity of the workers. It is also necessary to establish joint effluent treatment plants, particularly for small- and medium-sized enterprises, in industrial zones and ensure that all units meet government environmental regulations with regard to emissions and waste discharge systems.

Most waterways in Sri Lanka were polluted during the initial stages of rapid industrialization in the late 1970s and early 1980s. Due to this and the increased awareness of environmental protection, manufacturers in present-day Sri Lanka face stringent laws and regulations that require them to put in place expensive remediation mechanisms. This is an area where the state can initiate collective action, and given the strong producer networks in Sri Lanka, it seems to be easily forthcoming. The "win-win" benefits that result from such conformity to standards have been widely documented in the literature (refer to Khan et al. 2003).

Summary and Conclusions

Sri Lanka benefited, as did other South Asian countries, from the protective MFA and the tariff hopping it induced. While the RMG sector has performed creditably, successive Sri Lankan governments missed important opportunities or destroyed the ones that had been created. Thus, Sri Lanka was unable to capitalize on the initial growth of high-quality cotton and textile production. A misconceived protectionist policy in the 1970s threw out the baby with the bathwater when it blocked the imports of textile machinery and technologies. The demise of the textile industry also meant the demise of cotton production.

Sri Lanka liberalized early, relative to the rest of South Asia in the late 1970s, but another opportunity was missed when it solely focused higher up in the value chain on RMGs. The fallout is that the country relies on imports of most of the raw material needed for the sector, and the linkage potential downstream or upstream has not been explored. Reliance on imported inputs is a severe constraint in the garment industry, where fashions change rapidly and there is a premium on quick and reliable delivery.

As in all our case studies, manufacturers complained about inadequate business conditions that add to their cost of production. A comparative assessment of business conditions in South Asia suggest that, other than the high cost of electricity, they are generally better in Sri Lanka. However, there still is a role for industrial policy in certain areas, and the state needs to create the facilitating conditions by initiating and providing what the private sector will not, even as it demands high performance standards and competitive conditions.

Competition should not always be understood in conventional ways. One of the interesting findings of the Sri Lanka case study is the role of networking and social capital whereby firms of similar scales in the RMG sector cooperate with each other to meet delivery deadlines and in other ways. Other notable aspects of the Sri Lankan RMG sector include the flexible production methods adopted to meet quickly changing fashions in the garment sector and an active participation in global value chains to deliver higher-value garments. In an interesting case of South-South FDI, Pakistani competitors have been attracted by tax incentives to help reestablish the textile industry. However, the high level of production concentration and the lack of export diversification are issues of concern.

Annexure 7.1

List of Interviewees in Sri Lanka

Date (2006)	Name of company	Persons interviewed	Designations	Other information
July 6	Sanchia (Pvt.) Ltd.	Mr. G. M. Rameez	Manager, Marketing and Operations	
		Mr. W. Hannibal	Merchandise Manager	
		Mr. J. Davis	CEO	
July 12	Brandix College of Clothing Technology		CEO	Does not wish the name of the company or his name to be disclosed (mainly discussed general trends).
July 13	Favorite Garments (Pvt.) Ltd.	Mr. Anil Weerasinghe	Managing Director	
July 14	MAS Active (Pvt.) Ltd.		Marketing Manager	Does not wish the name of the company or his name to be disclosed.
July 15	Union Apparel (Pvt.) Ltd.	Mr. P. Mahiepala	CEO	
July 18	Nobles (Pvt.) Ltd.	Mr. S. Wettimuny	Vice Chairman	
July 18	Pride Ventures (Pvt.) Ltd.	Mr. W. De Silva	Managing Director	One of the many companies that had to be closed down due to high costs.
July 19	Avro Garments (Pvt.) Ltd.	Mrs. Bandusili	Supervisor	Small-scale company
July 19	Serendib (Pvt.) Ltd.	Mr. P. Pathiranage	Director	Small-scale company
July 21	Ranmalu Fashions (Pvt.) Ltd.	Mr. R. Mather	Director	
July 22	Hidramani Group of Companies	Mr. A. Ediriweera	Human Resources Manager	
July 26	Voguetex (Pvt.) Ltd.	Mr. S. Samraj	Director	
		Mr. L. P. Mendis	Chairman	
July 31	Desco Apparel Consulting Services	Mr. V. De Silva	Managing Director	
August 4	Brandix (Pvt.) Ltd.		Foreign Consultant	Does not wish the company name or the
			Merchandise Manager	name of the persons interviewed disclosed.

Annexure 7.2

Producer Associations in Sri Lanka

The apparel industry in Sri Lanka today is vibrant with every indication that this vibrancy will be sustained—especially with the more active participation of the government, including its specialized agencies like the Export Development Board, and with initiatives championed by the industry in association with the state and a host of microinitiatives taken by the individual members / units of the apparel industry.

Joint Apparel Associations Forum
The Joint Apparel Associations Forum (JAAF) was set up in November 2002 as an apex body to coordinate, sustain, and develop the apparel industry in Sri Lanka. Hitherto, the industry was regulated, or coordinated by a number of associations including the

- Sri Lanka Apparel Exporters Association
- Free-Trade Zone Manufacturers Association
- National Apparel Exporters Association
- Sri Lanka Chamber of Garment Exporters Association
- Sri Lanka Garment Buying Offices Association

Upon setting up the JAAF, all activities with regard to the smoother functioning of Sri Lanka's apparel industry are addressed by various implementation subcommittees of the JAAF, including

- Backward Integration
- Bilateral/ Multilateral Trade
- Human Resource Development
- Logistics
- Marketing/Image Building

All these subcommittees are headed by individuals with long experience in the trade. http://www.jaafsl.com/.

The National Apparel Exporter Association
The National Apparel Exporter Association (NAEA) was established in 1993, and its membership comprises enterprises, partnerships, sole proprietorships, and limited liability companies, carrying on business under the

200 Garment Factory Program in Sri Lanka and registered with the BOI. The primary objectives of the association are as follows:

- Promotion, fostering, and protection of the rights and privileges of its members.
- Establishment, maintenance, and conduct of a forum to resolve matters and affairs affecting its membership and rights, particularly in the garment sector.
- Representation on behalf of its members before government departments, institutions, and statutory bodies.
- Propagation and promotion of the interests of its members in the garment trade, which also briefly sums up the policy of this association.
- Communication through fortnightly e-mails and weekly news bulletins about the latest Textile Quota Board decisions, members requirements for quota exchange/transfers, and listing of redundant stocks with members (this is now redundant with the phasing out of the MFA).

Sri Lanka Chamber of Garment Exporters
The mission of the Sri Lanka Chamber of Garment Exporters (SLCGE) is to represent small- and medium-scale garment manufacturers at various forums to protect the interests of the sector. SLCGE was formed in 1992, at a time when the small- and medium-scale garment manufacturers were threatened with closure. The chamber was able to arrest this situation through the various representations it made to the government. It was solely due to the representations made by the chamber that the government introduced provisions in the rules for the allocation of textile quotas for permitting the small- and medium-scale manufacturers a minimum of 4,000 dozens of hot quota categories. There are over 450 manufacturers in both the small-scale and medium-scale sectors, and the chamber continues to look after their interests.

The chamber is now addressing its energies to getting government approval for the establishment of a restructuring fund, which is necessary for the small-scale sector to upgrade their machinery and factory to survive in the nonquota era.

Sri Lankan Apparel Exporters Association
Inaugurated in 1982, The Sri Lankan Apparel Exporters Association (SLAEA) is a pioneer association of the apparel export industry in Sri Lanka. A professional secretariat disseminates information promptly and speedily to its members, convenes regular meetings, and organizes seminars and workshops. In its 24-year history, the SLAEA has been a steadfast partner

of the government of Sri Lanka. The association serves on many statutory and nonstatutory boards/committees, chambers, and associations connected with the industry, and has contributed to the formulation and implementation of major strategies and decisions affecting the industry.

Sri Lanka Garment Buying Offices Association
The Sri Lanka Garment Buying Offices Association (SLGBOA) was formed in 1993 with the primary objective of promoting and fostering the growth of the garment industry in Sri Lanka. The members of the SLGBOA represent international prestigious brand names and are responsible for the generation of approximately 70 percent of Sri Lanka's exports of textiles and apparels. The membership represents all major global importers and retailers in the United States, European Union, Australia, and Japan. A majority of the association's membership has been carrying out operations in Sri Lanka for more than 8 to 13 years, marketing the country and its merchandise effectively. The association is also a strong lobby for the industry.

The organization purports to achieve the following for its members:

- Identifying potential manufacturers who adhere to stringent requirements as specified by the buyer (Bringing together compatible parties for mutual benefit).
- Providing service that exceeds customer expectations at a price that precludes competition.
- Supporting the manufacturing base with latest market information that will help them retain a competitive edge, thus improving the quality of the product.
- Providing inbound logistics through promotions.
- Providing samples, quality assurance, and quality checking.
- Providing support services such as procurement, technological inputs, infrastructure assistance, and human resource development.

PART III

Synthesis of Exporter Findings
and Importer Survey

Synthesis and Conclusion

This book has sought to explore the *processes* that explain the export success and the state of the RMG sector in South Asia, such as industrial policy; business, structural, and institutional factors; and various forms of linkages and partnerships including backward and forward (induced by industrial policy or spontaneous), public-private, domestic-foreign (in a value chain context), South-South, and intracluster or intrasector. While South Asian countries have, in keeping with the prediction of mainstream trade theory, specialized in this sector given their advantage in cheap labor and also in some cases the availability of raw materials, we sought to go beyond "what" (countries specialize in) to "why" (they select particular products), but more important "how" (this works in practice).

South Asian countries are part of a historical continuum, such that comparative advantage in garment production in Asia has continued to shift from the West to Japan, to the Asian Tigers (Korea, Taiwan, Singapore, and Hong Kong), to a new tier of South East Asian emerging economies (Malaysia, Thailand, Indonesia, and the Philippines), and finally to the most recent tier of such countries as China, Vietnam, and Cambodia. Thus, in a "flying geese" pattern, as some Asian countries confronted rising labor costs and moved up the value chain, others assumed leadership in garment production lower down the value chain.

South Asia might have had to wait longer had it not been for trade protection the West engaged in to prevent market disruption and the consequent unemployment the collapse of its labor-intensive garment sector would have resulted in. The protective trading regime (MFA), instituted first under GATT and then the WTO, assigned export quotas to countries, and this gave South Asia a market opening they might otherwise have had to wait for. The quotas created incentives both for domestic producers and for foreign investors seeking avenues for profitable exports when domestic quotas had been filled, a practice referred to as "quota hopping."

It was widely predicted that after the end of the MFA on January 1, 2005, most South Asian countries, barring India, would not be able to withstand the competition, particularly from China. While the dust has not yet settled, some aspects of the prediction have been realized. China has quickly grabbed a larger market share and might have been even more successful had it not been restrained by continued tariffs to prevent "market disruption" in its main markets in the United States and Europe, measures that China agreed to in its articles of accession to the WTO. This may have provided breathing room to its competitors until end 2008.

The Maldives textile industry has collapsed because of the trade liberalization following the MFA phaseout, and Nepal appears to have been very adversely affected. Pakistan and Sri Lanka have shown some weakness in one of the two markets cited above, either United States or Europe, but for the most part are doing well so far. Contrary to expectations, Bangladesh has forged ahead with robust export growth and, as expected, this has been more the case with India. We turn now to the processes, as described above, explaining export success viewed from the vantage point of businesses.

There are some commonalities in the responses across the board, and these are not surprising. As profit maximizers, businesses are wont to complain even when they are doing well, because their objective is to increase profits constantly. So the chorus of complaints about business conditions was universal. We showed in chapter 1 that this was with some justification, because the business environment needs improvement across the board, in terms of both infrastructure and the facilitative and regulatory environment. For example, Bangladesh has made tremendous progress, but is constrained by the bottleneck represented by inadequate port facilities.

Another commonality was that businesses were very reluctant to give any credit to government, and most attributed success to their own efforts, particularly their flexibility, and generally viewed the government as a hindrance. This appeared to be the case even when we were able to document an extensive facilitative role being played by the government via industrial policies of various kinds. The case for industrial policy was self-evident from the narratives of the businesspersons. Much of this case for industrial policy was premised on a perceived need for state intervention to facilitate coordination, that is, to induce forward and backward linkages within the industry and provide public goods where collective action would not be forthcoming. Nepal was not taking advantage of backward linkages, and this was also a shortcoming in Sri Lanka.

Linkages across sectors in the industry were more evident in knitwear than in the woven sector, and progress through linkages was most evident in Bangladesh. In Bangladesh, domestic accessories such as interlining, labels, buttons, zippers, drawstrings, and sewing thread, and packaging materials such as neck boards, backboards, plastic collar stays, tissue paper, hangtags, pins and clips, hangars, and polybags were traditionally imported, but by 2006, 70 percent of the demand was being met domestically. In the 1990s, value addition in the RMG sector was 20 percent, but this had risen to around 45 percent by 2006. With respect to the knitwear sector, about 85–90 percent of the raw material demand was being met by local knitting and knit-dyeing mills. For the woven sector, about 25 percent of the total demand for fabric was being met by local weaving and processing mills. The interviewees noted that the emergence of a female workforce with purchasing capacity led to an increased demand for products such as cosmetics and clothing. This, in turn, led to increased spending on advertising of these products, which mainly benefited television channels.

While our objective was not to engage in empirical exercises to estimate the quantitative impact of industrial policies, nonetheless the various industrial policy measures cited below were solicited and were likely to have helped. Industrial policy in India is perhaps the most extensive and one that spans the value chain. Projections showed that only 30 percent of the industry's need for long-variety cotton would be fulfilled domestically. The Technology Mission for Cotton was established to raise cotton productivity via various interventions, and the outcome was an increase in cotton yields by 57 percent from 2002 to 2006. Various more conventional fiscal policy measures were used to encourage production and exports. The Foreign Trade Policy of 2004 allowed for exemptions from import duties for key inputs like trimmings and embellishments. Export Oriented Units (EOU) were tax-exempt on export income and faced no import or export duty. Firms located in Special Economic Zones (SEZ) were given similar privileges.

There were also nontraditional and ambitious interventions, such as the Technology Upgradation Funds Scheme, providing subsidized medium- and long-term interest rates, and the Scheme for Integrated Textile Parks to encourage cluster development, so firms could benefit from external economies, and once the consolidation was achieved, to concentrate on providing world-class infrastructure via public-private partnerships. By 2007, 30 textile parks were approved with a government contribution of 40 percent of the total cost.

Again, using public-private partnerships, there has been a concerted attempt to redress the shortage of skilled labor in the garment sector. The government has been establishing industrial training institutes (ITIs) in more regions and has been using the existing ITIs and polytechnics in catchment areas to introduce textile- and garment-related courses. The Apparel Export Promotion Council is running over a dozen training and design centers and has plans to establish two-dozen additional centers. Also, one-time grants are being awarded to the private sector to set up such institutes or build in-house capacity.

A shortcoming for the RMG sector in India has been the low level of FDI. For example, in 2005, the total FDI in this sector in India was 1.8 percent of the total ($79 million) compared with 8.3 percent ($5.4 billion) in China. The government has engaged in a concerted effort to redress this situation with an action plan that includes targeting countries and firms with the potential to invest, participating in international fairs and summits to project India as an FDI destination, and addressing the operational problems that might be deterring such investment.

Bangladesh's industrial policy had an innovative feature of "back-to-back" letters of credit that provided virtually unlimited working capital to even small- and medium-sized enterprises for export related production. The government's encouragement of backward linkages into textiles production (yarn and fabric) with generous cash incentives for exported garments made from domestically produced yarn and fabric was similarly innovative. Other measures were more conventional, such as the creation of bonded warehouses for duty-free imported inputs for garment exports.

Under Pakistan's trade policy of 2003, three "garment cities" were established, all with SEZs privileges, but also designed to function like industrial clusters with many horizontal linkages. The government had offered lucrative rebates to garment manufacturers, which amounted at times from 12 percent to 15 percent of total cost. In addition, the government reduced the regulatory duty on polyester chips and waived regulatory duty on industrial sewing machines, knitting machines and spares, and other export-related textile materials and machinery. This facility of duty-free imports enabled the garments sector to become established and modernized and the technology to be diffused. Warehousing facilities were enhanced, since this was also viewed as a constraint.

A research and development subsidy was put in place, although, despite much lobbying by businesses, it was not extended in the 2008–2009 budget on grounds that it would run afoul of WTO trade rules. The Trade Development Association of Pakistan, a more politically correct name for the Export Promotion Bureau in the WTO era, undertook to enhance technology, brand development, and brand marketing.

The government has also been extensively involved in training efforts in partnership with the private sector. It first initiated the RMG technical training institutes, but moved to on-the-job training schemes when it was realized that workers could not avail themselves of the regular technical training being provided since they could not afford to take time off from work. A Sewing Operators Training Program provided three months' training on the job with the government paying 50 percent of the salary for the duration. The Textile Garments Skill Development Board was set up in 2005 and had been training between 22,000 and 22,500 new trainees per year. The trainees were receiving a stipend of Rs. 2,500 per month, and the board was contributing Rs. 1,000 as trainer fee. 75 percent of the seats were reserved for women. A Stitching Machine Operator Training scheme was launched in June 2006 in which selected garment factories were declared as training institutions.

Sri Lanka also pursues an active industrial policy despite its liberal stance. Exporters registered with the Board of Investment become eligible for tax holidays or preferential rates and for custom duty and foreign exchange exemptions. The unique aspect of this policy is that for registered firms, the policy is binding on all future governments.

In fact, when explaining Nepal's inability to sustain its export success into the post-MFA period, the unwillingness of the government to engage in an active industrial policy, apart from the country's landlocked status, stands out. Other factors that might account for Nepal's poor performance include political instability and rigid labor market conditions. However, Bangladesh's RMG sector became more dynamic post-MFA, despite much political instability; Pakistani exporters have held their own despite political insecurity, and India has forged ahead despite labor market rigidities. Nepali entrepreneurs took advantage of incentives created by the MFA quotas and so should be equally capable of taking advantage of a targeted industrial policy that rewards success.

South-South linkages were not an issue we set out to explore, but we came across several examples of them. For example, India has invested in Egypt to take advantage of lower tariffs on the latter's garment exports to the U.S. market. Sri Lanka had engaged in the training of workers from Bangladesh and opened units in places like Bangladesh, Maldives, Jordan, Kenya, and Mauritius to enhance its garment delivery capacity. Pakistani industrialists are engaged in foreign direct investment in Sri Lanka, to the chagrin of the Pakistani textile producer association, to develop the Sri Lankan textile industry, given their greater experience down the production chain in yarn and fabric manufacturing. Interestingly, this linkage was an outcome of protectionist EU policy that extended duty-free import privileges to Sri Lanka but with stringent rules of origin. Pakistani businesses were drawn with generous incentives to establish textile mills, and this could finally jump start Sri Lanka's backward linkage to textiles. India, which had quota-hopped and set up establishments in Nepal during the MFA era, is now subcontracting work to Nepal to avail itself of cheaper labor.

At times, the lead (apex) firms in the value chain located in the West have facilitated the shifting of production units on a temporary basis within South Asia. For example, production was shifted from India to Bangladesh to meet specified costs per unit on a consignment when production conditions changed in India. Firms are willing to bear a temporary loss to maintain a reputation for timely delivery. In India, lead firms of the value chain also promoted links between domestic firms to improve the coordination of different functions in the chain, such as dyeing and coloring. It is likely that, across the board, these links will grow, even though all countries and firms operate in a fiercely competitive environment. It brings to mind the cooperative-competitive framework A. K. Sen used to analyze interspousal relations within the household decision-making context.

While business linkages within South Asia were a surprise, local-foreign partnerships were expected and were indeed very much in evidence, particularly in Sri Lanka. Sri Lanka has moved up the value chain via such linkages and by developing a flexible production capacity, so much so that machinery can be quickly retooled to accommodate changing product lines as fashions change. There was widespread acknowledgment that foreign partnerships represented a source of equity and capital and transfer of technology, market information, and quality standards.

We found that the hoped for transfer and diffusion of technology has often occurred. Thus, Bangladesh started with a partnership agreement, and senior management's setting up enterprises and labor mobility's passing on skills resulted in the technological diffusion. Pakistan seeks and has benefited from joint ventures, but this has been less evident in Bangladesh than we expected, although not for the lack of interest on the part of entrepreneurs. We attribute the reluctance of firms to set up production facilities to the lack of political stability which makes the more arm length interaction via governance of the value chain, rather than establishing domestic operations, a safer bet.

The links with the lead firms in the value chain are facilitating the introduction of standards, both labor and environmental, across the board. Thus, while the governments vociferously complain that these represent non-tariff barriers, change is already under way in the South Asian firms that are engaged in a global value chain. In Pakistan, there were examples of small-scale units losing orders because of a lack of compliance. Businesses in both Bangladesh and Sri Lanka complained about the different codes of conduct imposed by their different partners, and so there is a need for buyer firms to recognize international standards, rather than insist on their own "codes of conduct."

The links among firms within the industry were also explored and were found to exist in various forms in Sri Lanka, India, and Bangladesh. Sri Lankan firms operated in a thick network of associations: both informal, via a shared background among managers and business leaders, and formal, via industrial associations. This social capital facilitated the use of another firm's capacity or the sharing of orders in a crunch. Bangladeshi firms were less close-knit, but there was evidence of sharing capacity with or subcontracting to others to deliver on a large order.

In India, firms shared capacity and jointly hired professional lobbyists to influence policy. There was also evidence of other forms of cooperation in the competitive framework in India. For example, to enable firms further up the chain to win international bids, firms lower down in the chain conceded input price cuts. Similarly, to help with successful bidding, firms higher up in the chain helped those lower down in the chain with technology and process upgrading. India was unique in demonstrating interindustry links. For example, one RMG company engaged in joint research with chemical companies and a nanotechnology firm to develop innovative "wrinkle-free" shirts and trousers, in which they are market leaders, and which command a premium in the international market.

Clusters are able to build synergies and negotiate for services. For example, whereas one power-loom unit can only make a limited range of products on its own, it is possible to make a wide range of items in apparel parks. Firms share not only production capacity but also embroidery facilities. Again, individual power-loom units, which lack assets and markets, are able to become bankable, attain creditworthiness, and benefit from economies of scale when they come together as consortiums in apparel parks.

Thus, apparel parks and clusters have helped overcome structural deficiencies of smaller individual manufacturing units in India. This is most apparent in the case of the Tirupur cluster, which has been adopted by UNIDO as a model. The Tirupur Exporters Association has cooperated on a range of projects including common effluent treatment plants, industrial parks, an exhibition center, integrated textile parks, and a fashion institute. In this case, the fact that the entrepreneurs are from the same ethnic community of Goundars enabled the cluster networking to benefit from and be reinforced by the embodied social capital.

In Pakistan, manufacturers have engaged in collective action mostly for winning concessions from the government, and in this regard the industry lobbies are very active. The export figures at the end of the quarter or year often belie the crisis they claim the industry or sector is in. Historically, the industry collectively sought and acquired support in crises, but given that it claims to be in perpetual crises, the government appears to have become less responsive. Although the government effectively rewarded success in allocating quotas during the MFA regime, Pakistan's economic bureaucracy, in general, still does not appear to have learnt the fine art of rewarding success and ignoring failure that the East Asian economies so effectively practiced as part of their industrial policy.

Characterizing the overall country experience in a nutshell is difficult, but one interpretation of the evidence is as follows: Bangladeshi manufacturers, while seeking state support, demonstrate a much greater degree of self-reliance and boldness. Their thrust has been toward knitwear, given the greater potential for value addition and backward linkages. Most countries have been able to diversify, but Bangladesh is notable in using acquired skills to push ahead very dynamically. India is making solid progress, and it is already a major player and will continue to be, given its vast labor reserves. It is developing its own brands, and it now has the muscle, as other industries, to acquire technology by buying Western corporations and brands and is doing so. Pakistani business has been and continues to be very cautious. Its comparative advantage seems to be in the woven sector, given its particular brand of cotton. Despite massive industrial policy initiatives referred to above, manufactures keep up a deafening roar for more support to avoid disaster, even though the performance statistics belies this fear. It seems that getting over years of crony capitalism is difficult. Security concerns have frightened away foreign investors, and bringing them back is likely to continue to be a challenge for a while. Sri Lanka has moved up the value chain and is skillfully serving niche markets, such as lingerie, and is in the process of establishing backward linkages. Nepal's RMG sector appears to be in the greatest trouble and may be able to reverse the problem by focusing on a partnership with India.

Even for a market system, the world economy changed very rapidly in 2008. Initially, with food prices rising, there was upward wage pressure. Fuel prices impacted the RMG sector in terms of higher cost of production, but more importantly due to higher costs of transportation. Subsequently, the financial crisis in the US and its fallout resulted in recessionary conditions globally. Beyond challenging short term market fluctuations, South Asian countries will face long term market challenges in maintaining the low-cost advantage that drove the expansion of their exports. It may be wise to rapidly cultivate the various linkages referred to above and to simultaneously explore domestic markets and other markets closer to South Asia, including Africa and the Middle East. To rely exclusively on the traditional markets in the West is unlikely to be a winning strategy in the long term.

Appendix

Importer Survey

The empirical chapters of this book (chapters 3–7) explore the RMG (readymade garment) sector in the five most populous South Asian countries to identify the processes, particularly the various forms of linkages, accounting for successful RMG exports and the constraints to this success. During the fieldwork, we came across cases of South Asian firms located in global value or commodity chains (GVC) or engaged in joint ventures or other forms of partnership with European or U.S. firms.

We decided therefore to survey importers in the United States to get the buyers' perspective of one of South Asia's largest markets. Using GVCs as a conceptual framework (refer to section 1.3), we wished to provide the perspective from the apex or control centers of the value chains. The specific purpose of the chapter was to examine both successful and failed RMG importer/exporter trade partnerships and identify lessons for making the partnerships more effective.

Our original research design was to solicit contacts of foreign partners from the exporters, particularly of those based in the United States, and then interview the importers to get their perspective on what accounts for their success and what might be the constraints for an exporter. In all the South Asian countries, we were unsuccessful in acquiring the contacts of foreign partners from the exporting firms. This is not surprising since in an intensely competitive business environment, foreign buyers are a closely guarded trade secret.

We revised our research design and decided to solicit interviews from the major players in the U.S. RMG importing. To our surprise, we found these firms to be equally, if not more, cagey in agreeing to one-on-one interviews, and this is despite the fact that we approached these firms through contacts who had present or past links with them. We conjectured that this wariness may have been caused by the bad press that some firms receive from investigative coverage of the use of child labor by their partner exporters or negligence of other forms of corporate responsibility on their part, and also because, like exporter firms, they seek to protect information that might be of value to competitors.

We persisted and developed a set of research questions for importer interviews that is attached as Annexure I. While it is good to proceed with open-ended research questions in one-on-one interviews to avoid the risk of excluding important information that close ended questionnaires pose, we had to convert these questions into much more structured questionnaires (Annexure II) for the mail-in survey, since respondents are generally willing to devote a very limited time to them. The electronic version entirely ruled out open-ended questions.

The questionnaires are quite innocuous, but that notwithstanding, U.S. RMG importers proved to be unresponsive at best and evasive at worst. Of the 70 importers contacted, only one actually responded, and we had to abort our attempt at writing a chapter based on importer survey responses. This appendix documents the process used to elicit responses and the lessons learnt for the benefit of other potential researchers.

As is the standard practice in survey research, we started with creating a sampling frame that included parent companies of all the major U.S. department and clothing stores. The final count came to 70 major RMG importers, and we decided to survey all of them. The first point of contact was through their websites. We sent e-mails requesting a personal interview with employees conversant with RMG importing. We sent our request through customer service, since contact information for corporate head-quarters were generally not available.

Of the 70 importers contacted, only three responded. The first was an automatic response assuring us of additional contact in two hours—the contact never occurred, much less in two hours. The other two responses stated that company policy prohibited interviews on proprietary topics and deferred to the companies' respective student research web pages—neither of which was particularly informative in answering our questions.

After waiting for a month, it became clear that email contact would not garner the kind of responses necessary for the chapter's completion. Personal contacts were initiated with four major U.S. importers who were sent a copy of the survey. Our hope was that a few in-depth interviews might still provide adequate insights pertaining to the research. Unfortunately, the interviews were not granted and the surveys were never completed. The legal teams in each of the four companies eventually overruled our personal contacts in order to protect proprietary information. This process of negotiating for possible interviews took another three months.

As communication through the Internet and verbal communication through contacts failed, we spent the next month trying to establish written communication. Headquarter addresses—often obtained from investor, not customer, websites—were added to the initial sampling frame and a mass mailing list was prepared. The mailing list included a copy of the letter attached as Annexure III, a copy of the questionnaire in Annexure I, and a prestamped return envelope for survey responses. In the following month, only two U.S. importers responded. One declined and the other indicated their willingness to complete the survey via a phone interview. However, the interview never occurred, as the contact person remained continuously unavailable or out-of-town.

One month after the first mailing, a second letter was sent to the same U.S. importers as a reminder. This was our last attempt, urging the 70 importers to complete an online version of the survey. We hoped that the increased efficiency and anonymity of an online survey would generate more responses. Unfortunately, only one importer completed the survey, and so we were unable to write the chapter on the U.S. importers' perspective.

Over the course of seven months, the primary barrier to pertinent survey responses was corporate reports. As long as the company in question had a public report on environmental and labor standards, it felt justified in denying our requests for additional information. Supporting this denial of our requests and simultaneously forming a second barrier to information were the U.S. importers' legal departments. Although competition renders some safeguards necessary, "proprietary information" effectively became the legal euphemism for "response denied." Even when the survey managed to bypass the public relations reports and corporate legal departments, it became mired in a third information barrier, company bureaucracy. In a sea of departments, hierarchies, meetings, and answering machines, survey responses could be, and were, postponed indefinitely. Thus the barriers to survey responses were formidable.

Future researchers in this field may gain from our experience by doing the following: First, pay closer attention to the language used when contacting potential respondents. For example, one company responded negatively to our use of the term "low-income countries." We changed this in subsequent mailings to an even more neutral "South Asian countries." Second, in the RMG sector, U.S. importers tend to inform their investors more than their customers. In other words, it may be worthwhile finding the company's investor website for more informative reports and useful contacts. Finally, engage U.S. importers in the research process as early as possible. Using this study as an example, we infer that importers might have felt more comfortable completing the survey questions had they actually participated in formulating the questions. However, the introduction of corporate culture into academic research might be questionable. Our final recommendation is that perhaps survey research should be abandoned and more effort should be made via networking to secure half a dozen or so open-ended and in-depth interviews.

Annexure I

Importer Research Questions

What in your view accounts for the success of a low-income country exporter?

What in your view accounts for the failure of a low-income country exporter?

Are you satisfied with your partnership with the exporters? Please explain.

What mechanism would you recommend to the exporters for making the partnership with your company more effective?

What do you anticipate as the future of this partnership?

Why did you decide to work with companies in low-income countries? (If your company has a production association with the exporter)

Have you done anything to assist exporters with any of the following:

- Technology
- Management assistance
- Quality control
- Marketing assistance
- Funds
- Other

Is the final product you import part of a value chain, and if so, do you monitor the whole chain? Please explain.

Do you require exporters to conform to a code of conduct? If so, is this based on:

- Social standards?
- Environmental standards?
- Other?

Do you confront any nontariff barriers or hindrances to importing? Please explain.

Is there any other issue that you think we should document?

Annexure II

Importer Mail-In Questionnaire

What are the main problems you face in the exporting country? (Please circle yes (Y) or no (N))

1. Delays Y/N
2. Poor quality Y/N
3. Discrepancy between sample and delivery Y/N
4. Lack of conformity to specified standards Y/N
5. Other, please specify

If there are delays, what are the main causes?

1. Bureaucratic hurdles in getting clearances Y/N
2. Corruption Y/N
3. Poor infrastructure Y/N
4. Poor port facilities Y/N
5. Other, please specify

What in your view defines a successful low-income country exporter?

Have you done anything to assist exporters with any of the following:

– Technology Y/N
– Management assistance Y/N
– Quality control Y/N
– Marketing assistance Y/N
– Information technology for better communication Y/N
– Funds Y/N
– Other, please specify

Do you require exporters to conform to a code of conduct? Y/N

If yes, what is the code comprised of?

– Quality standards Y/N
– Management standards Y/N
– Social standards Y/N
– Environmental standards Y/N
– Other, please specify

What mechanisms are employed to achieve the results desired by your firm?

- In-house branch for supervision Y/N
- Utilizing intermediaries Y/N
- Utilizing information technology Y/N
- Other

What mechanism would you recommend for making the partnership more effective?

What are the main problems, if any, you face in your home country?

1. Bureaucratic problems Y/N
2. Government not viewing imports as conforming to standards Y/N
3. Delays in the ports Y/N
4. Other, please specify

Any other issue that you think we should document?

Annexure III

Importer Mail-In Letter

MOUNTHOLYOKE.

Mount Holyoke College
Department of Economics
50 College Street, South Hadley, MA 01075-1481
tel 413-538-2432   fax 413-538-2323
econ@mtholyoke.edu

Date

Dear Company Name,

Mount Holyoke College is funding a study to explore successful readymade garment (RMG) exporting from South Asian countries. Such South Asian trade with the United States has assumed great importance after the repeal of the MFA (Multi-Fiber Arrangement) on January 1, 2005.

An essential part of this study, which will be published by Palgrave Macmillan, will be based on responses to the attached value-neutral survey. Our objective is to garner U.S. retail industry perspectives on what factors contribute to a successful or an unsuccessful importer/exporter partnership in RMG trade. In order to best achieve this objective, we are currently soliciting responses from all major U.S. department and retail store chains engaged in importing from South Asia.

We hope that the results of our study will facilitate the garment trade by providing important information on establishing and maintaining effective RMG partnerships. We also hope to identify the possible constraints to such trade and the appropriate policy responses. This study is unique in its approach that takes into account perspectives of both importers and exporters for being sensitive to production realities.

We value your perspective and welcome your insights and will be happy to share our findings with you, should you so desire.

Thank you for your time and assistance in this endeavor.

Sincerely,

Shahrukh Rafi Khan
Visiting Professor of Economics
Mouth Holyoke College
khans@mtholyoke.edu

Courtney Van Cleve, Co-author
cavancle@mtholyoke.edu

Notes

Chapter 1

1. See section 1.2.
2. Trade data is classified at various levels of aggregation based on a code such as that of the United Nations Harmonized System (HS). More numbers in the code represent a greater product disaggregation. Thus, for example, the six-digit HS code 620111 represents men's and boys' overcoats of wool or hair, not knit. Finer disaggregation would require moving to a higher code, say to the eight-digit or even the ten-digit level.
3. Linkage is defined much more broadly than the original use of this term by Hirschman (1958).
4. The "textile industry" refers to knit or woven fabric (made from natural or synthetic fibers, filaments, or yarn) converted into clothing. Woven fabric is spun using a process of "warp and weft" that follows a horizontal and vertical pattern. Woven fabrics have a higher thread count and therefore are generally more costly to produce than knitwear. In the apparel sector, knitwear is popular for making women's and children's clothing, whereas for men's apparel woven fabrics are in demand. Woven items include, for example, cotton shirts and denim items, while knitwear items include, for example, polo shirts and T-shirts. Clothing, apparel, or garments are used broadly and interchangeably and made-ups (for example bed linen) or hosiery is not excluded. RMG is referred to as a sector rather than an industry since it is part of the textile industry.
5. The RMG sector as part of the broader textile industry is presented in a historical context in chapter 2.
6. For a detailed review refer to Choi and Hartigan (2005).
7. Some of the more academic points are relegated to footnotes and the general reader could ignore them.
8. More technically, nonspecialization followed from constant returns to scale (which followed from having labor as the only factor) being replaced with decreasing returns. There is also an important ideological break in the move from classical to neoclassical theory in that underlying Adam Smith's and David Ricardo's theorization was that labor was the only source of value and that other factors acquired their value by the amount of labor that was embodied in them to bring them to the market.

9. These include decreasing returns to scale but also other assumptions regarding tastes, technology, and the utilization of resources.

10. Another strand in the literature, Krishna (2005) and Mavroidis (2005), is preferential trade agreements that include customs unions, regional free trade agreements, bilateral agreements across regions, and multilateral agreements.

11. The classic works in this regard are by Leontief (1954, 1956).

12. Other explanations for trade between countries at similar income levels could include transportation costs, other location advantages, and seasonal variations.

13. "New trade theory" models, Helpman and Krugman (1985) and Levinsohn, Deardorff, and Stern (1995), represent the more formal relaxation of the stringent assumptions of the HO model to address real world conditions such as imperfect competition and increasing returns to scale.

14. These would include external economies available to first movers that result from firms conferring benefits on each other. For example, providing to each other inputs not otherwise easily available or providing them at lower cost, knowledge, technology, trained labor, and other services. This positive dynamic makes catching up more difficult.

15. Refer to Ocampo (1986) and Dutt (1988).

16. This theory was therefore subject to the same criticism as Marx's analysis with regards to transforming value into prices. For an overview see Bieri (2007).

17. For a historical account indicating that this was the path to industrialization for current HICs refer to Chang (2002) and for an attempt to empirically measure dynamic efficiencies of industrialization refer to Khan, Bilginsoy, and Alam (1997).

18. Refer to Deraniyagala and Fine (2006) for a heterodox critique of the orthodox case for "free-trade."

19. Baldwin (2006) provides a useful exposition and extension of this approach. Baldwin argues that the first unbundling was the movement of goods that resulted from a fall in transport costs and the second, currently under way, has resulted from information technology and a fall in the costs of communication. The first may well be reversed with the rise in energy costs, and this is likely to impact the second.

20. Unit labor cost is the wage bill divided by labor productivity and is the relevant measure of the competitiveness. Thus cheap labor is not enough for nations to be competitive in world markets, although it can on occasion compensate for low productivity.

21. This review draws on Khan and Kazmi (2008).

22. The pioneering work is Gerrefi (1994). More recent work relevant to this chapter includes Gerrefi (1998), Gerrefi (1999), Gereffi (2000), Gereffi (2000a), and Bair and Gereffi (2001). The exhaustive handbook for value-chain research by Kaplinsky and Morris (www.ids.ac.uk) is a good resource for researchers in this field as is the Web site. Henderson et al. (2002) proffered a network approach to analyzing global production.

23. Kenny and Florida (1994) also emphasize this aspect of GVC analysis in their work.
24. Also refer to Edginton and Hayter (1997) and Kaplinsky and Moris (2002) for other classifications.
25. For a more detailed classification and account of governance mechanisms, with "the complexity of transactions, the ability to codify [them] and the capabilities of the supply-base" playing a central role, refer to Gereffi, Humphrey, and Sturgeon (2005).
26. This could be viewed as "full package" delivery compared to sewing precut inputs or engaging in CMT (cut-make-trim). Cammett (2006, p. 35) mentions that lead firms even pass on functions such as packaging (to get floor ready merchandize) and warehousing on to suppliers to cut costs.
27. Cammett (2006, p. 35) refers to electronic data interfaces that enable close product monitoring.
28. The alternatives are completely hands-off market transactions or production by subsidiaries or joint ventures.
29. Other scholars have written on the distribution of this value across the chain and the ability of firms from low-income countries to move to higher value production. Our focus here is much more limited.
30. Meso refers to the middle ground between micro and macro, and the focus is on structural and institutional issues.
31. Refer to Irwin (2005, p. 32).
32. Refer to Amsden (1989), Wade (1990), Rock (1995), and Rodrik (2006) for the impact of industrial policy on exports in various contexts. Refer to Adhikari and Weeratunge (2007, p. 135) for a specific account of industrial policy used to encourage the textile and clothing sector in South Asia in a comparative context. India's industrial policy interventions appear to be the most extensive and Nepal's the least.
33. Porter (1990) has an exhaustive account, based on industry studies, of export success of particular industries in different high-income countries.
34. Schumpter (1934) more broadly viewed innovative entrepreneurs in this context.
35. Referred to as a "historical accident" by Krugman (1991).
36. This brief historical account is drawn from Ghani (1996, p. 8). The working paper is also available from http://ravi.lums.edu.pk/cmer/upload/Sialkot_enterprenurial_Spirit.pdf.
37. Refer to Nadvi (1999). In 2007, the Pakistani government was being called upon to undertake similar efforts on behalf of fishery exports to the EU.
38. This account is drawn from Rhee (1991). Also refer to Rahman (2004).
39. For more details refer to chapter 3.
40. This paragraph is drawn from Nadvi and Halder (2002). Also refer to Nadvi and Schmitz (1994) for an account of industrial clusters.
41. Refer to Fafchamps and Minten (2002) for social capital in an industrial context.

42. Two sets of questionnaires are annexed to this chapter as Annexure 1.1 and 1.2. The third, meant for importers, is reported in the Appendix to the book in the context of documenting our failure to get an adequate response rate to write a chapter on importers' perspectives.
43. http://www.comtrade.un.org or www.untrains.com.
44. Often growth rates were astronomical, but from a very small quantity in the base year and to a very small export weight in the terminal year. Such industries and products were therefore not selected, although their performance might be markers for future successes.
45. Rodrik (2008) points out that there is implicitly the presumption of one uniformly successful business model underlying the criteria in Table 1.6 and that may just not be the case.

Chapter 2

1. The textile industry played a central role in the first phase of the Industrial Revolution in Britain with the various technical and mechanical innovations that tremendously boosted productivity. These included the Flying Shuttle (1733), Spinning Jenny (1764), Water Frame (1764), Spinning Mule (1779), and Power Loom (1785). For the central role of the cotton textile industry in the Industrial Revolution, refer to Deane (1979, pp. 97–102).
2. This pattern of international production restructuring was developed as a descriptive model and referred to as the "flying geese" paradigm by Akamatsu (1962). While it applies more generally to shifting patterns of industrialization internationally, the textile and clothing industry is a very good example of its application.
3. Since the division of South Asia into nation-states occurred in 1947, prior to this year the subcontinent is referred to as India.
4. The original group of countries "NIC" referred to included Korea, Taiwan (China), Hong Kong, and Singapore, also referred to as the East Asian Tigers. Emerging economies is now a broader term that also includes, inter alia, Malaysia, Indonesia, Thailand, and China.
5. Ramaswamy and Gereffi (2000, p. 194) point out that apparel became the leading export sector for all four East Asian NIEs.
6. Anderson (1994) also documents this shifting pattern of production consistent with the flying geese model.
7. For an example of such partnership between Desh, Bangladesh, and Daewoo, Korea, refer to sections 1.4 and 3.4.
8. This included farmers, spinners, weavers, and merchants.
9. Development economists rediscovered the importance of agglomeration, referred to as clusters, in the late twentieth century. See for example Schmitz (1997).
10. These company servants were often vicious and exploitative and served their own ends in cahoots with company employees (p. 110).
11. Wallerstein (1974).

12. Chaudhuri (1996, p. 75) points out that the availability of abundant skilled labor and the obvious technical superiority of the Indian textile industry was unlikely to create the motivation for an industrial revolution in India. Beyond that, the other initial conditions such as governance concerned with commercial and public interest, infrastructure, and adequate capital markets were not present. For Britain, among other scientific, institutional, and economic processes under way, offsetting the comparative advantage of the Indian textile industry was a likely motivation.
13. Refer to endnote 1.
14. Cypher and Dietz (2004, p. 79) report a 70 to 80 percent tariff on textile imports from India and zero duty on raw cotton.
15. Grey cloth is the term that is applied to woven and knitted fabrics and is synonymous with "loomstate," which refers to the condition in which the woven cloth leaves the loom.
16. Keesing and Wolf (1980).
17. Refer to Krishna and Tan (1998) and Hale (2000).
18. Nordus (2004).
19. The latest numbers reported at the time of writing (mid-2008) for COMTRADE and TRAINS, which report exports to all countries, were for 2004. Maldives is not reported to have exported to either of these markets and so its garment sector was a casualty of the MFA phaseout. This is confirmed by Adhikari and Weeratunge (2007, p. 117), who report that even in 2003, textiles and clothing represented a third of Maldives' total merchandize exports.
20. Adikari and Yamamoto (2005). Vietnam's joining the WTO on January 2007 poses another challenge.
21. Adhikari and Weeratunge (2007, p. 112) point out that despite these advantages Eastern Europe, Mexico, and the Caribbean have been losing market share post the MFA phaseout.

Chapter 3

1. Like India, Bengal, the eastern part of which is now Bangladesh, was an important center for textile manufacturing and trade under the East India Company. Thus the region that is currently Bangladesh has a rich precolonial and colonial history of textile production, as narrated in chapter 2.
2. Ahmed and Hossain (2006).
3. Bangladesh Garment Manufacturers and Exporters Association (BGMEA), http://bgmea.com.bd/.
4. World Bank (2006). Various studies have examined the positive social impact that accompanies the inclusion of such a huge number of women in the labor force in a conservative low-income country. Refer for example to Kabeer (2004).
5. This figure is an approximation because the labor force of 76.76 million for 2004 that was obtained from the World Resources Institute Web site.

(http://earthtrends.wri.org/text/economics-business/variable-841.html on June 11) is not for a comparable year.

6. Chowdhury (2003).
7. Islam (1994).
8. World Bank (1995).
9. Banglapedia, Garment Industry http://banglapedia.search.com.bd/HT/G_0041.htm.
10. USITC (2004).
11. Banglapedia, Garment Industry http://banglapedia.search.com.bd/HT/G_0041.htm.
12. Ibid.
13. World Bank (2006).
14. Ibid.
15. Within the EU, Germany, UK, France, and Belgium are major destinations for Bangladesh's apparel exports.
16. Ahmed and Hossain (2006).
17. Ibid.
18. Mlachila and Yang (2004, p.7) report that about 90 percent of the factories are located in or close to Dhaka and Chittagong.
19. This is also indicated to be the case for Nepal, Pakistan, and Sri Lanka (see chapters 5, 6, and 7).
20. OECD (2004).
21. As explained in OECD (2004), the fragmentation of the supply chain was further advanced as high-income countries consented to preferential trade arrangements (known as production-sharing arrangements or outward-processing programs) with a few low-income countries. These arrangements led to the textiles or precut materials being exported into low-income countries for final assembly, and the finished clothing products were then reimported to high-income countries under preferential provisions referred to as the GSP or Generalized System of Preferences. The qualifications stipulating where inputs are to be purchased from are referred to as rules of origin (ROO). Bangladesh enjoys preferential access under the European Union Generalized System of Preferences (EU GSP) scheme, which provides Bangladesh with zero-tariff access to EU markets. For a description of the GSP and the associated ROO pertaining to the raw materials used for the final products refer to http://trade.ec.europa.eu/doclib/docs/2004/march/tradoc_116448.pdf.
22. Reaz Garments, that changed its name to M/s Reaz Garments in 1973, was the first direct exporter of garments from Bangladesh (http://banglapedia. search.com.bd/HT/G_0041.htm).
23. Due to quota ceilings, apparel export by Daewoo Corporation of Korea became constrained. Thus, Daewoo became interested in Bangladesh, since Bangladesh had unutilized quotas that would enable Daewoo to "quota hop" and also find a market for its capital equipment. In exchange, Daewoo agreed to provide training in technical and marketing skills. For details and references, see 1.4.

24. http://banglapedia.search.com.bd/HT/G_0041.htm.
25. This is akin to the use of the term "nimble fingers" by entrepreneurs as a pretext for hiring young girls or children in, for example, carpet weaving, as identified in the feminist economics literature. Refer to Elson (1996, pp. 35–55).
26. The qualifier "possible" is used because one is not holding quality constant.
27. Back-to-back letters of credit (L/C) are used in international and domestic trade. The main parties to a back-to-back L/C are the buyers and their bank as the issuer of the original L/C; the sellers/manufacturers and their bank; and the manufacturers' subcontractor and their bank. This type of credit transaction is used when a seller/manufacturer has to purchase a component or subcontract part of the manufacturing of a product, but may not have the cash flow to do so. In such a situation, the sellers/manufacturers apply to their bank for an L/C identical to the original L/C received from the buyer, except that it is for a lesser value. This second L/C, called a back-to-back L/C, is sent to the subcontractor's bank and therefore the subcontractor knows that they will be paid and can proceed with their part of the transaction, that is, supply of components or services to the manufacturer. Back-to-back L/C provides small- and medium-sized exporters virtually unlimited working capital to finance their sales and be a party to more export related transactions. For an alternative interpretation of back-to-back L/C to the one we received from the field, that is, as one that represents an onerous restriction, refer to Mlachila and Yang (2004, p. 23).
28. Mlachila and Yang (2004, pp. 23–25) also mention a duty drawback scheme and reduced income tax rates, but suggest that corruption and poor implementation are likely to have made them ineffectual. Khan (2000, p. 31) contends that conventional liberalization policies as part of structural adjustment programs, including deregulation and exchange rate, financial sector, and fiscal reforms, helped the sector by creating a favorable macroeconomic environment.
29. Under the military-backed caretaker government, political agitations such as hartals have been banned, but it remains to be seen if such a policy will stay in place when a democratically elected government is once again in power.
30. The exchange rate during the time of the fieldwork was approximately Tk. 59 to a dollar.
31. http://www.towerfreight.com/ocean.html.
32. Daily Star (Dhaka), 2006, "Chittagong Port Congestion: Capacity Needs to be Built to Handle Rising Trade," Tuesday April 25.
33. With the development of the container system for carrying cargo, the Chittagong and Mongla ports virtually became feeder ports. In the past, export-import cargo was carried by the ships in bulk. However, the development of transport technologies worldwide has led to the replacement of the bulk ships by container ships. The container mother vessels, which have a capacity of around 10,000–20,000 containers, do not dock at Bangladesh's ports. They anchor at the seaports in Singapore, Malaysia, or Sri Lanka. The Bangladesh-bound container cargo is first unloaded at these ports and later

carried up to Chittagong and Mongla by feeder vessels (which are vessels that are part of a cargo network in which the larger and faster vessels only call at the major ports at both ends of the area being covered, and the smaller ports are served by the smaller feeder vessels that transfer the cargo to and from the major port terminals). The export cargo in containers from Bangladesh is transported the same way. About 50 feeder vessels dominate the routes between Chittagong-Mongla and ports in Singapore, Malaysia, and Sri Lanka. Most of the feeder vessel operators are foreigners. It is alleged that a Singapore-based syndicate of ship owners controls the feeder operation on this route. In the past there have been tensions between RMG exporters and feeder operators over imposition of congestion surcharges. Source: http://www.thedailystar.net/forum/2007/february/window.htm.

34. Bangladesh's highly competitive export performance may have accounted for this.
35. According to World Bank (2006), Bangladeshi exporters have been lobbying Congress for duty-free access to the U.S. market under a proposed bipartisan bill named Tariff Relief Assistance for Developing Economies (TRADE) Act 2005.
36. http://www.shamunnay.org/download/post_mfa_era.pdf.
37. The calculation is based on data obtained from the BGMEA. Also refer to Mlachila and Yang (2004) for the dramatic growth of knitwear in the early part of the decade.
38. Quasem (2002).
39. Ibid.
40. As cited in Quasem (2002).
41. Ibid.
42. Banglapedia, Garment Industry, http://banglapedia.search.com.bd/HT/G_0041.htm.
43. Ibid.
44. World Bank (2006). A field visit to a knitwear factory also confirmed the degree of integration in the knitwear sector. The knitwear factory manager also claimed that in the knitwear sector manufacturers had more flexibility and room for creativity as they could supply buyers their own designs and fabric. Thus it is not surprising that the degree of value addition would be higher in the knitwear sector.
45. Ibid.
46. Ibid.
47. Hossain, T. G. K. M., 2006, "Textiles profile: tradition, modernity and competitiveness," *The Daily Star Investment* (Dhaka), February 16.
48. http://banglapedia.search.com.bd/HT/G_0041.htm.
49. Strict compliance has a positive side in that ensuring better working conditions potentially boosts productivity and certification provides access to more markets.
50. http://www.southasianmedia.net/conference/conference_envisioning/vision_goup_xiv.htm.

51. Countries such as Jordan, Egypt, and Mexico that have free trade agreements with the United States enjoy duty-free access for textiles. However, given the asymmetrical power of the potential partners, these agreements have to be carefully negotiated so that the weaker partner to the agreement does not sign away much more than it is getting.

Chapter 4

1. Government of India (2006a).
2. Export-Import Bank of India (2005).
3. Those interested in the broader literature on textiles and garments in India could consult RoyChowdhury (1995), who reviews the problems of the industry in the 1980s, Ramaswamy and Gereffi (2000), who explore the Indian garment industry, including the industry after the 1991 reforms, in a value chain context, and Chadha et al. (2005), a comprehensive report that explores the state of the industry up to the phasing out of the MFA.
4. Chadha et al. (2005).
5. Government of India (2006a).
6. Table 2.3 comes to the same conclusion using data for importing countries.
7. Government of India (2006a).
8. Chandra (2006).
9. Export-Import Bank of India (2005).
10. Chandra (2006).
11. UN TRAINS (2007).
12. Annexure 4.1 lists interviewees, and Table 1.3 provides the breakdown by respondents.
13. At least part of this gap can be explained by business motivations and limited government resources. Profit maximizers always want more and the government has limited resources, and competing demands, and is driven, when all works well and often it does not, by the broader national interest.
14. Government of India (2006a).
15. Ibid.
16. Ibid.
17. Chadha et al. (2005).
18. Uchikawa (1999) in Chadha et al. (2005).
19. Refer to section 2.3 for India's historical strength in textiles.
20. Government of India (2006a).
21. Interview with Mr. Hinduja, Managing Director, Gokaldas Images.
22. Chadha et al. (2005).
23. Interview with Mr. Mehta, Managing Director, Creative Outwear Ltd.
24. Refer to subsections 4.4.4.1 and 4.4.4.2.
25. Interview with Mr. Mehta, Managing Director, Creative Outwear.
26. Interview with Mr. Hariharan, General Manager, Sonal Garments.
27. Interview with Mr. Narayanan, Sr. Manager (Exports), Alok Industries Ltd.

162 • Notes

28. Interview with Mr. Javeri, President, Madura Garments.
29. Ibid.
30. Interview with Gunish Jain, Director, Royal Embroidery.
31. Gokaldas Images (2006).
32. Interviews with Mr. Hinduja, CEO Marketing, Gokaldas Exports, and with Mr. Javeri, President, Madura Garments.
33. Interview with Mr. Javeri, President, Madura Garments.
34. Interview with Mr. Hinduja, Managing Director, Gokaldas Images.
35. Government of India (2006a).
36. Ibid.
37. Export-Import Bank of India (2005).
38. Interview with Mr. Javeri, President, Madura Garments, and Mr. Hinduja, Managing Director, Gokaldas Images.
39. Interview with Mr. Hinduja, CEO Marketing, Gokaldas Exports.
40. Interview with Mr. Narahari, Chief of Marketing, Madura Garments.
41. Interview with Mr. Javeri, President, Madura Garments.
42. Government of India (2006a).
43. Ibid.
44. Ibid.
45. Interview with Mr. S. Hariharan, General Manager, Sonal Garments.
46. Interview with Mr. S. Hariharan, General Manager, Sonal Garments.
47. Ibid.
48. Verma (2002).
49. Chadha et al. (2005).
50. Kathuria and Bhardwaj (1998).
51. Government of India (2006a).
52. Ibid.
53. Interview with Mr. D. L. Sharma, President, Vardhaman Textiles Ltd.
54. EXIM Bank (2003).
55. Interview with Mrs. Dhar, General Manager, Indo Polycoats Ltd.
56. Panthaki (2003).
57. Interview with Mr. Rahul Mehta, Managing Director, Creative Outwear.
58. Ibid.
59. Interview with Mr. D. K. Nair, Secretary General, Confederation of Indian Textile. Industry (CITI), Delhi.
60. Interview with Mr. Mehta, Managing Director, Creative Outwear.
61. South Asia Watch on Trade, Economics and Environment (2004).
62. Centad (2006).
63. Government of India (2006a).
64. Interview with Mr. Jain, Director, Royal Embroidery.
65. Interview with Mr. Sharma, President, Vardhaman Textiles.
66. Interview with Mr. Nair, Secretary General, Confederation of Indian Textile Industry (CITI).
67. Interview with Mr. Sharma, President, Vardhaman Textiles.

68. Interview with Mr. Puri, Managing Director, Marshal Overseas Pvt. Ltd.
69. Interview with Mr. Srinivasan, Head, Reliance Retail Apparel Business, Reliance Industries.
70. Interview with Mr. Puri, Marshal Overseas, and Mr. Srinivasan, Head, Reliance Retail Apparel Business, Reliance Industries.
71. Economist Intelligence Unit (2008).
72. Preetha (2007) in *Hindu*, August 5, 2007. Of late, the rupee has been depreciating, and it declined from Rs. 39.9 on March 8, 2008, to Rs. 42.8 on June 29, 2008, for $1.
73. Interview with Mr. Ramananda, Senior Manager, K. Mohan & Company.
74. Interview with Mr. Kesar, Director, Okhla Garments and Textiles Cluster.
75. Okhla Garments and Textiles Cluster.
76. Interview with Mr. Sakthivel, Chairman, Poppys Group, and President, Tirupur Exporters Association.
77. Refer to chapter 1.3 for more details and citations.
78. Apparel parks are commercial industrial parks, usually developed as public-private partnerships (PPP) with manufacturing units for multiple textile firms and processes.
79. Interview with Mr. Sakthivel, Chairman, Poppys Group, and President, Tirupur Exporters Association.
80. Interview with Mr. Shanmugam, Director, the Great Indian Linen and Textile Company Ltd.
81. The exchange rate of the Indian rupee for $1 was about 39.4 at the end of 2007.
82. Interview with Mr. R. M. Subramaniam, Consultant, Cluster Development Initiative, IL&FS.
83. Interview with Mr. A. Sakthivel, Chairman, Poppys Group, and President, Tirupur Exporters Association and Mr. P. Shanmugam, Director, the Great Indian Linen and Textile Company Ltd.
84. Interview with Mr. R. C. M. Reddy, Director, Cluster Development Initiative, IL&FS.
85. Interview with Mr. Subramaniam, Consultant, Cluster Development Initiative, IL&FS.
86. Ibid.
87. Government of India (2006a).
88. Interview with Mr. Khullar, Director (Textiles), Planning Commission of India.
89. Interview with Mr. Narendra, Indus Fila, Bangalore.
90. Okhla Garment and Textile Cluster (OGTC) newsletter.
91. "First-tier" mills have spinning units to make yarn whereas "second-tier mills" refer to vertically integrated composite mills that have weaving, knitting, and processing units.
92. Interview with Mr. Dhamotharan, Madura Garments.
93. Interview with Mr. Dhamotharan, Madura Garments.

94. Interview with Mr. Narahari, Chief of Marketing, Madura Garments.
95. Interview with Mr. Jagadish Hinduja, Managing Director, Gokaldas Images. Refer to Ramaswamy and Gereffi (2000, p. 194) for a fuller list of importers (value chain apex companies) in the United States.
96. Ibid.
97. Interview with Mrs. Dhar, General Manager, Indo Polycoats Ltd.
98. Interview with Ms. Meera, Manager, Cascade Enterprises.
99. Interview with Ms. Meera, Manager, Cascade Enterprises, Bangalore.
100. Interview with Mr. S. Hariharan, General Manager, Sonal Garments, Bangalore.
101. Interview with Ms. Sheetal Jambhale, Merchandiser, Alok Industries Ltd. Bombay.
102. Interview with Mr. S. Hariharan, General Manager, Sonal Garments, Bangalore.
103. Government of India (2006a).
104. Interview with Mr. Srinivasan, Head, Reliance Retail Apparel Business, Reliance Industries.
105. Refer to subsection 4.4.4.1 for government initiatives in this regard.
106. Government of India (2006a).
107. Interview with Mr. Javeri, CEO, Madura Garments.
108. Government of India (2006a).
109. Government of India (2007).
110. Free on board (FOB) means that all expenses to the ship are covered, in addition to loading costs. However, this does not include freight, insurance, unloading costs, or transportation at the importing destination.
111. Ibid.
112. Government of India (2007).
113. Interview with Mr. Mehta, Managing Director, Creative Outwear.
114. Government of India (2006a).
115. Ibid.
116. Meeting with Mr. Anand, Director, BKS Textiles Private Ltd., Palladam.
117. Interview with Mr. Vivek Hinduja, CEO Marketing, Gokaldas Exports.
118. Interview with Mr. R. C. Jhamtani, Adviser, Planning Commission of India.
119. Interview with Mr. R. M. Subramaniam, Consultant, Cluster Development Initiative, IL&FS.
120. Government of India (2006).
121. Interview with Mr. Khullar, Director (Textiles), Planning Commission of India.
122. Interview with Mr. B. S. Sinha, Director, Cotton Division, Ministry of Textiles.
123. Government of India (2006a).
124. Interview with Mr. Dash, Adviser (Industry), Planning Commission of India.
125. Government of India (2006a).
126. Ibid.

127. Interview with Mr. Nair, Secretary General, Confederation of Indian Textile Industry (CITI).
128. Interview with Mr. Sakthivel, Chairman, Poppys Group and President, Tirupur Exporters Association.
129. The authors find these demands excessive. The 1935 ILO 40-hour workweek convention came into force in 1957 as indicated on the ILO Web site, http://www.ilo.org/global/lang–en/index.htm.
130. Interview with Mr. D. K. Nair, Secretary General, Confederation of Indian Textile Industry (CITI).
131. Interview with Mr. M. S. Ramananda, Senior Manager, K Mohan & Company (Exports) Pvt. Ltd.

Chapter 5

1. These were HS 610910 (T-shirts, singlets, and other vests of cotton, knit) and HS 620462 (women's and girls' trousers and shorts of cotton, not knit).
2. Ms. Pradhananga was also involved in the UNDP-SAWTEE project titled "Addressing the Impact of the Phasing Out of Textiles and Clothing Quotas on Nepal." This chapter has immensely benefited from the findings of the survey for the UNDP-SWATEE project that consisted of interviews with garment exporters and present and former garment workers. Ms. Pradhananga had the opportunity to actively participate in various discussion and seminars related to the garment sector under the project. The chapter has gained from presentations of and interactions with the persons listed 7–13 in the list of interviewees in Annexure 5.1.
3. Garment Association Nepal (GAN), www.ganasso.org.
4. SWATEE (2006).
5. GAN.
6. Government of Nepal, Ministry of Finance, *Economic Surveys*, various issues.
7. Nepal Rasta Bank (NRB), various issues.
8. SAWTEE (2006).
9. UNCTAD (2004).
10. NRB, various issues.
11. Table 2.3, which uses a different source and reports data until 2007, affirms this finding.
12. The following example illustrates the difficulties faced by RMG entrepreneurs in such an unstable political environment. During a six-day strike that began on March 6, 2007, in the eastern Terai (the plains on the southern part of the country bordering India) region, the major customs points through India were blocked, including the Birgunj-Raxaul and Rani-Jogbani. These two custom points account for over 45 percent of Nepal's export/import activities. Due to the strike, 150 cargo containers were stranded in various parts of the country for a week.
13. Nepal's largest garment exporter, Cotton Comfort, closed down production in December 2006 due to rapid deterioration in the industrial environment.

Cotton Comfort exported US$9 million worth of RMGs in 2005–2006, accounting for about 18 percent of the country's total garment export. However, it shut down after increased politically affiliated trade union activity.

14. Government of Nepal, (2004).
15. Shakya (2005).
16. Refer to section 4.4.4.3 of this volume for reduced lead times in India.
17. Chang (2006), pp. 47–52.
18. Adhikari (2006).
19. Under the financial assistance of the World Bank, the government of Nepal has established ICDs in the three major transit points of the country: Biratnagar, Bhairahwa, and Birgunj. The first two are road-based ICDs and the third is rail based and linked directly with Kolkata in India.
20. Shakya (2005).
21. Ibid.
22. Lezama, Webber, and Dagher (2004).
23. Stringent ROO may require "substantial transformation" of a product, and it may not be considered as belonging to the exporting country if it has a high content of imported raw material.

Chapter 6

1. This information is drawn from the subsection on RMG in the "manufacturing, mining and investment policy" chapters in various recent issues of the *Pakistan Economic Survey* and from Government of Pakistan, 2006, *Economic Survey 2005–2006*, Economic Advisors' Wing, Finance Division, Islamabad. The estimate is provisional.
2. Editor's page, 2004–2005, "Garment Exports in Quota-Free World" *Pakistan Textile Journal*, http://www.ptj.com.pk/. Seigmann (2005, p. 402) calculated that women constituted about 30 percent of the workforce in the textile and clothing industry, compared with a national average of 15 percent.
3. Government of Pakistan (2005).
4. Manjur (2002).
5. Ibid.
6. In early 2007, the name of the Export Promotion Bureau was changed to the Trade Development Authority of Pakistan.
7. Ramadan is the holy month of fasting, based on the Muslim lunar calendar, when practitioners abstain from eating and drinking from sunrise to sunset, and others often follow suit because of social pressure.
8. Akhtar (2005).
9. Information provided by Mr. Asif Riaz Tata, Chairman of Naveena Exporters (Pvt.) Ltd., Karachi, Pakistan.
10. The allocation of quotas in Pakistan was on the basis of performance, that is, the high performers received allocation of quotas equal to the actual quantity exported by them under each category during the preceding year to a specific quota country. This made the quota allocation 100 percent dependent on the

past performance, that is, success was rewarded. Quotas could also be sold by one firm to another. Government policy in Pakistan was replicating, in this regard, East Asian industrial policy of rewarding success [Wade (2004)]. However, unit price realization was not accorded any consideration in quota allocations. In addition, the government auctioned the growth quotas and the residual quotas available to it under bilateral arrangements with the quota countries to earn revenue. There were no provisions for allocation in the existing quota policy for potential investors and new entrants in the apparel and textile business. Also, the strategy of building quotas resulted in excessive specialization. For the nuances of quota policy and policy changes refer to Manjur (2002, pp. 174–176).

11. Manjur (2002).
12. Ibid.
13. Interview with the garment indenter Mr. Atiq Kochra.
14. Recall from chapter 3 that there was no such hesitation in Bangladesh.
15. Mr. Ghulam Mohammed, Managing Director at Globe Managements (Pvt.) Ltd., claimed that on average Pakistani manufacturing units produced eight shirts per day per machine, whereas Bangladesh produced seventeen shirts and Sri Lanka twenty-five. Asif Merchant, speaking on behalf of S. M. Traders, claimed that while Pakistani manufacturers were aiming for 20–28 pieces per machine, South Asian competitors were aiming for 38–45 pieces per machine, and that Pakistani manufacturers had almost a 30 percent higher cost of production than competitors. Mrs. Ulrike Qureshi, Director of Texflow Buying Services that deals with small-scale units on behalf of European buyers, explained that repeated mistakes in dyeing and printing were made in small-scale units, and even one mistake meant that the entire cloth is wasted. She provided a conservative estimate of a wastage rate of between 15 and 20 percent. We have been unable to verify this information independently, although all industrialists and government officials interviewed acknowledged the wastage and inefficiency problems plaguing the industry.
16. The sources cited in the table suggest that price, rather than quantity, fluctuations, account for the big swings in percentage growth.
17. Contaminated cotton has been noted by the government to be a particularly serious problem (2007, p. 38), and the federal government has launched a Clean Cotton Program in collaboration with the Trading Corporation of Pakistan and provincial government agricultural departments. The program includes paying a premium of Rs. 50 per maund (82.28 lb) directly to growers, as an incentive for cleaner cotton.
18. As in endnote 1.
19. Some interviewees claimed that their sales representatives made eight to ten trips a year, and that this increased the cost of production by 6 percent.
20. Newspaper articles documented the demand for travel support made by the PRGMEA. See for example http://paktribune.com/business/newsdetail.php?nid=885.
21. This confirms the contention of industrialists that marketing costs due to travel is adding to their costs of production.

22. In the budget of 2008–2009, the government announced that the subsidy would be withdrawn because it had run a foul of WTO rules.

23. Various other government-assisted institutes in Karachi include the Textile Institute of Pakistan, S. M. A. Rizvi Textile Institute, Fashion Apparel Design & Training Institute, and PHMA Institute of Knitwear Technology. Those in Lahore include Pakistan School of Fashion Design and Pakistan Knitwear Training Institute.

24. Textile Garments Skill Development Board, Ministry of Textile Industry, Government of Pakistan. http://www.pakistan.gov.pk/ministries/index.jsp?MinID=40&cPath=602.

25. The source of this information was the interview with Mr. Atiq Kochra, the Manager of Rubytex.

26. The average exchange rate between July 2005 and April 2006 was Rs. 59.81 for $1, Government of Pakistan, Economic Survey, Statistical Annexure (2006, p. 86).

27. Nusrat (2005).

28. Government of Pakistan (2006).

29. These numbers may also indicate the limitations of relying solely on perceptions. Comparative data reported in Table 1.6 had over twice as many firm managers viewing electricity as a worse business constraint in Bangladesh than in Pakistan. It could be that Pakistani managers had already become more used to self-generation of electricity.

30. In early March 2007, the government rejected demands from a delegation of textile industrialists to provide more subsidies and stated that the industry itself needed to become more competitive. That notwithstanding, industry associations have kept up a crescendo of demands, and it appears that newspaper stories of the impending crisis and the inability of Pakistani entrepreneurs to succeed without government support may have been planted. See http://thenews.jan.com.pk/daily_detal.asp?id=46367.

31. Government of Pakistan (2006).

32. The indemnity bond protects the lender, in this case the government, in case of a shortfall in repayment.

33. The Tycoon International, 2006, "Textiles: the Spine of Pakistan's Economy," August–September, p.16 and Table 2.3.

34. We were unable to independently verify this, except for the cash subsidy in Bangladesh, and similar claims have been made for example by garment manufacturers in the other South Asian countries in the other case studies in this volume.

35. Hummels (2001) estimated the costs of delays in transport, such as those associated with customs clearance, at 1 percent per day. Refer to Tables 1.6 and 1.7 for a detailed review of the comparative business environments across the five South Asian countries. Bangladesh is shown to be most wanting in the perception of business managers and in terms of objective data on regulation.

36. Gupta et al. (2006).

37. Journal for Asia on Textile & Apparel (ATA Journal), October–November 2006, http://textile.2456.com/JasperWeb/industry/lang-eng/ind-4/index.aspx.

38. For more recent numbers refer to Table 2.3 and Annexures 2.2 and 2.3, which show that Pakistan's RMG sector has managed to continue to expand exports to its main markets up to 2007. The exception has been a 15 percent decline in export growth to the EU in articles of apparel and clothing accessories, knitted or crocheted, between 2004 and 2007.

39. Government of Pakistan (2004).

Chapter 7

1. As in Bangladesh, by the later 1990s, a high proportion of the workers in the RMG sector were women. They accounted for 87 percent of the workforce but only 16 percent of senior management (Kelegama 2002, p. 201).

2. Short- and long-sleeved shirts were manufactured using cotton and synthetic not-knit material.

3. J. E. F. Fernando, a textile technologist who has worked in the textile industry and the RMG sector for the past 40 years, provided invaluable information for this and the other sections. In addition, we have heavily relied on Kelegame (2005), and Kelegama and Epaarachchi (2002) for this section.

4. Several student/young professional insurgencies against the earlier government had been put down during the early part of the 1970s, and the new government did not want to trigger such movements. Refer for example to Cooper (2003).

5. Kelegama (2002, p. 198).

6. For example, the Katunayake FTZ was established in 1978. According to the Government of Sri Lanka (2003), the FTZs have been the recipient of the inflow of foreign direct investment into Sri Lanka and the linchpin of economic development. Kelegama (2005, p. 54) reported that at the turn of the century, FDI accounted for 50 percent of the ownership of garment factories and 50 percent of the exports.

7. Kelegama (2002) pointed out that 65 percent of material inputs were imported.

8. Kelegama (2005).

9. Ibid., p. 56.

10. Ibid.; also refer to Table 2.3.

11. This information was procured from the Joint Apparel Association Forum (JAAF), http://www.jaafsl.com/. It is confirmed by importer data reported in Annexures 2.2 and 2.3, although Sri Lanka posted a negative growth of 20 percent to the U.S. market in the "articles of apparel and clothing accessories, not knitted or crocheted" category.

12. Kelegama (2005, p. 55). This is much the same as East Asian economies moving to Sri Lanka to take advantage of the lower unit costs in the 1970s. At the turn of the century, Sri Lanka relocated the RMG production to other countries to take advantage of the U.S. Trade and Development Act meant to encourage imports from the Caribbean and sub-Saharan Africa. Since it had

generous ROO (rules of origin) provisions for the first four years, Sri Lankan entrepreneurs took advantage of these provisions.

13. The list of interviewees is reported in Annexure 7.1.
14. Although the UNCTAD TRAINS data set we used suggested that HS 620469 (women's and girls' trousers, shorts, materials, not knit) is the top commodity category in Sri Lanka's exports to the rest of the world, the manufacturers we interviewed pointed out that this category is far outweighed by women's lingerie at the time of the interviews.
15. All factories we visited were situated in and around the capital city of Colombo.
16. The exchange rate in July 2006 was SLR 104 for US$1.
17. The BOI is designed to facilitate investment and operates as an autonomous statutory body. When an agreement is signed with the BOI, a company or individual may be eligible for tax holidays or preferential tax rates and exemption from customs duty and foreign exchange controls. The most attractive feature for investors is that the provisions of the agreement are honored by succeeding governments.
18. Since Sri Lanka is a small country with mutually acquainted professionals moving in similar circles, the networking and reciprocal obligations they operate on work intensely and effectively.
19. See Annexure 7.2 for a list of associations.
20. Table 1.6 suggests that these costs are perceived as a constraint by more managers in Sri Lanka than in India or Pakistan, but much less than in Bangladesh.
21. It is unclear why the market has failed to seize this opportunity.
22. Manufacturers also claimed, though we were unable to verify this, that the social and environmental codes of conduct imposed by buyers varied from country to country, and that they were very high and stringent. We suspect hyperbole in such claims and were exposed to similar complaints across all the South Asian countries covered in this volume.
23. Eighty-five percent of the roads in Sri Lanka are paved, compared with 9.5 percent in Bangladesh, but quality may still be a problem (refer to Table 1.5).
24. Overall, business conditions in Sri Lanka are more favorable than in the rest of South Asia, and even China (refer to Tables 1.6 and 1.7).
25. Refer to Kelegama (2005, p. 56) for historical and existing government efforts.
26. http://www.emergingtextiles.com/?q=art&s=060410Smark&r=free&i=samplearticle.
27. Refer to Khan (2007).
28. Interview with Mr. Anil Weerasinghe.
29. During this period, it was more profitable to import the textiles required for the RMG sector, as the textile mills were running at a loss and had to close down due to poor productivity. At the time, the government was more interested in promoting short-term business investment than in reviving the textile industry.
30. While some scholars argue that the space for such industrial policies have been closed, others like Amsden (2005) and Chang (2006) argue that notwithstanding WTO trade rules, low- and middle-income countries still have wiggle room.

References

Adhikari, R., 2006, "Governments' Support to the Textiles and Clothing Sector in Select Asian Countries," Report submitted to the UNDP Regional Bureau for Asia and the Pacific (unpublished draft), Colombo: UNDP Asia Pacific Regional Centre, Colombo.

————, and C. Weeratunge, 2007, "Textiles and Clothing Sector in South Asia: Coping with Post-Quota Challenges," http://www.undprcc.lk/Publications/TRADE/Centad_Yearbook_T_and_C_Chapter_RA_CW.pdf.

————, and Y. Yamamoto, 2005, "Flying Colours, Broken Thread: One Year of Evidence from Asia after the Phase-Out of Textiles and Clothing Quotas," Tracking Report, UNDP Regional Centre, Colombo, Sri Lanka.

Ahmed, M. N., and M. S. Hossain, 2006, "Future Prospects of Bangladesh's Ready-Made Garments Industry and the Supportive Policy Regime," Policy Analysis Unit (PAU), Research Department, Bangladesh Bank, Head Office, Dhaka, Bangladesh.

Akamatsu K., 1962, "A Historical Pattern of Economic growth in Developing Countries," *Journal of Developing Economies*, Vol. 1, No. 1.

Akhtar, M., 2005, "Cotton Production in Pakistan and the Role of Trading Corporation of Pakistan in Price Stabilization," Trading Corporation of Pakistan, Government of Pakistan, Islamabad.

Amsden, A. H., 1989, *Asia's Next Giant: South Korea and Later Industrialization* (New York: Oxford University Press).

————, 2005, "Promoting Industry under WTO Law," in *Putting Development First: The Importance of Policy Space in the WTO and International Financial Institutions*, ed. K. P. Gallagher (London: Zed Books).

Anderson, K., 1994, "Textiles and Clothing in Global Economic Development: East Asia's Dynamic Role" in *Managing Restructuring in the Textile and Garment Subsector: Examples from Asia*, ed. S. D. Meyanathan (Washington, D.C: World Bank).

Arasaratnam, S., 1996, "Weavers, Merchants and Company: The Handloom Industry in Southeastern India, 1750–90," in *Cloth and Commerce: Textiles in Colonial India*, ed. T. Roy (New Delhi: Altamira).

Bair, J., and G. Gereffi, 2001, "Local Clusters and Global Chains: The Causes and Consequences of Export Dynamism in Torreons's Blue Jeans Industry," *World Development.* Vol. 29, No. 11.

Baldwin, R., 2006, "Globalization: The Great Unbundling(s)," http://www.vnk.fi/hankkeet/talousneuvosto/tyo-kokoukset/globalisaatioselvitys-9-2006/artikkelit/Baldwin_06-09-20.pdfc.

Bhattacharya, D., and M. Rahman, 2000, "Bangladesh's Apparel Sector: Growth Trends and The Post-MFA Challenges." A paper presented at the National Seminar on Growth of Garment Industry in Bangladesh: Economic and Social Dimensions, the Bangladesh Institute of Development Studies, Dhaka, Bangladesh, July 21–22, 2000.

Bieri, D., 2007, "The Transformation Problem: A Tale of Two Interpretations," http://mpra.ub.uni-muenchen.de/3895/.

Cammett, M., 2006, "Development and the Changing Dynamics of Global Production: Global Value Chains and Local Clusters in Apparel Manufacturing," *Competition and Change*, Vol. 10, No. 1.

Centad (Center for Trade and Development), 2006, "Multilateralism at Cross-Roads: Reaffirming Development Priorities," *South Asian Yearbook of Trade and Development 2006* (New Delhi).

Chadha, R., D. Pratap, P. Sharma, and A. Tandon, 2005, "Indian Textiles: Weaving a Success Story," *Margin*, Vol. 37, No. 4 (National Council of Applied Economic Research).

Chandra, P., 2006, *The Textile and Apparel Industry in India* (Ahmedabad: Indian Institute of Management).

Chang, H., 2002, *Kicking Away the Ladder: Development Strategy in Historical Perspective* (London: Anthem).

Chang, H. J., 2006, *The East Asian Development Experience: The Miracle, the Crisis and the Future* (London/Penang: Zed Books/Third World Network).

Chaudhuri, K. N., 1978, *The Trading World of Asia and the English East India Company: 1660–1760* (Cambridge: Cambridge University Press).

———, 1996, "The Structure of Indian Textile Industry in the Seventeenth and Eighteenth Centuries," in *Cloth and Commerce: Textiles in Colonial India*, ed. T. Roy (New Delhi: Altamira).

Choi, E. K., and J. Hartigan, eds., 2005, *Handbook of International Trade*, Vol. I & II (Malden, MA: Blackwell).

Chowdhury, A., 2003, "International Competitiveness of Bangladesh Garments and Its Implication for the MFA Phase Out," A paper presented at the Bangladesh Institute of Development Studies (BIDS) Seminar Series, Dhaka, Bangladesh, June 18, 2003.

Cooper, T., 2003, "Sri Lanka, since 1971," Indian Subcontinent Database, http://www.acig.org/artman/publish/article_336.shtml.

Cypher, J. M., and J. L. Deitz, 2004, *The Process of Economic Development*, 2nd ed. (London: Routledge).

Deane, P., 1979, *The First Industrial Revolution* (Cambridge: Cambridge University Press).

Deraniyagala, S., and B. Fine, 2006. "Kicking Away the Logic: Free Trade Is Neither the Question Nor the Answer for Development," in *The New Development Economics: After the Washington Consensus*, eds. K. S. Jomo and B. Fine (New Delhi/London: Tulika Books/Zed Books).

De Soto, H., 2000, *The Mystery of Capital: Why Capitalism Triumphs in the West and Fails Everywhere Else* (New York: Perseus Book Group).

Dutt, A. K., 1988, "Monopoly Power and Uneven Development: Baran Revisited," *Journal of Development Studies*, Vol. 24, No. 2.

Economist Intelligence Unit, 2008, www.eiu.bvdep.com.

Edgington, D. W., and R. Hayter, 1997, "International Trade, Production Chains and Corporate Strategies: Japan's Timber Trade with British Colombia," *Regional Studies*, Vol. 31, No. 2.

Elbehri, A., T. Hertel, and W. Martin, 2003, "Estimating the Impact of WTO and Domestic Reforms on the Indian Cotton and Textile Sectors: A General Equilibrium Approach," *Review of Development Economics*, Vol. 7, No. 3.

Elson, D., 1996, "Appraising Recent Developments in the World Market for Nimble Fingers," in *Confronting State, Capital, and Patriarchy: Women Organizing in the Process of Industrialization,* eds. A. Chhachhi and R. Pittin (New York: St. Martin's).

Emmanuel, A., 1972, *Unequal Exchange: A study of the Imperialism of Trade*, trans. of Emmanuel 1969a by B. Pearce (New York & London: Monthly Review Press).

Export-Import Bank of India, 2003, "Transaction Costs of Indian Exports: A Review," Working Paper No. 4, Mumbai.

———, 2005, "Textile Exports: Post MFA Scenario – Opportunities and Challenges" (Mumbai: E Export-Import Bank of India).

Fafchamps, M., and B. Minten, 2002, "Returns to Social Network Capital among Traders," *Oxford Economic Papers*, Vol. 54, No. 2.

Garment Association of Nepal (GAN), www.ganasso.org.

Gereffi, G., 1994, "The Organization of Buyer Driven Global Commodity Chains: How U.S. Retailers Shape Overseas Production Networks," in eds. G. Gereffi and M. Korzeniewicz, *Commodity Chains and Global Capitalism* (Westport, CT: Praeger).

———, 1998, "Beyond the Developmental State: East Asia's Political Economies Reconsidered," in *More than the Market, More than the State: Global Commodity Chains and Industrial Upgrading in East Asia*, eds. S. Chan, C. Clark, and D. Lam (New York: St. Martin's Press), pp. 38–59.

———, 1999, "International Trade and Industrial Upgrading in the Apparel Commodity Chain," *Journal of International Economics*, Vol. 48, No. 1.

———, 2000, "Beyond the Producer-Driven/Buyer–Driven Dichotomy: An Expanded Typology of Global Value Chains, With Special Reference to the Internet," Duke University, draft.

———, 2000a, "The Transformation of the North American Apparel Industry: Is NAFTA a Curse or a Blessing," *Integration and Trade*, Vol. 1, No. 11.

Gereffi, G., J. Humphrey, and T. Sturgeon, 2005, "The Governance of Global Value Chains," *Review of International Political Economy*, Vol. 12, No. 1.

Ghani, J. A., 1996, "Sialkot's Entrepreneurial Spirit," Center for Management and Economic Research, Lahore University of Management Sciences, Working Paper No. 96, Lahore, Pakistan.

Gokaldas Images, 2006, *Creativity without Borders*, Gokaldas Images brochure, Bangalore.

Government of India, 2006, *Economic Survey 2005–2006*, Economic Advisor's Wing, Finance Division, New Delhi.

———, 2006a, "Report of the Working Group on Textiles and Jute Industry for the Eleventh Five Year Plan (2007–2012)," Ministry of Textiles, New Delhi.

———, 2007, *Annual Report 2006–2007*, Ministry of Textiles, New Delhi.

———, 2007, *Economic Survey 2006–2007*, Economic Advisor's Wing, Finance Division, New Delhi.

Government of Nepal, Ministry of Finance, *Economic Survey*, Kathmandu, Nepal, various issues.

———, 2004, "Nepal Trade and Competitiveness Study," Ministry of Industry, Commerce and Supplies (MOICS), Katmandu, Nepal.

Government of Pakistan, *Economic Survey*, Economic Advisor's Wing, Finance Division, Islamabad, various years.

———, 2004, *Foreign Trade Statistics*, Federal Bureau of Statistics, Islamabad.

———, 2005, SMEDA (Small and Medium Enterprise Development Authority), "Garments and Made-Ups (Textile)," www.smeda.org/business-development-7sector-briefs.html.

———, 2006, Export Promotion Bureau, "United States General Imports of Textile and Apparel Products Monthly Data by Country of Origin and Category Data in Category Units and U.S Dollars," Islamabad.

———, 2006a, Textile Garments Skill Development Board, Ministry of Textile Industry, http://www.pakistan.gov.pk/ministries/index.jsp?MinID=40&cPath=602.

———, 2007, *Economic Survey 2006–2007*, Economic Advisor's Wing, Finance Division, Islamabad.

Government of Sri Lanka, 2003, Board of Investment, http://www.boi.lk/InvestorSite/content.asp?content=about5&SubMenuID=36.

Grossman, G. M., and E. Rossi-Hansberg, 2006, "The Rise of Offshoring: It's Not Wine for Cloth Anymore," http://www.kc.frb.org/PUBLICAT/SYMPOS/2006/PDF/Grossman-Rossi-Hansberg.paper.0728.pdf.

Grubel, H. G., and P. J. Lloyd, 1975, *Intra-industry Trade: The Theory and Measurement of International Trade in Differentiated Products* (New York: Macmillan).

Gupta, R. A., P. Bhatiani, R. Yadav, and L. H. Mittal, 2006, *Quota Free World: A Year Later*, Technopak Study, www.technopak.com.

Hale, A., 2000, "Phasing Out the Multi Fiber Arrangement: What Does It Mean for Garment Workers?" Women Working Worldwide, Briefing Papers, Manchester, England, http://www.poptel.org.uk/womenww/phase_out_mfa.htm.

Hashim, D. A., 2005, "Post-MFA: Making the Textile and Garment Industry Competitive," *Economic and Political Weekly*, Vol. 40, No. 2.

Hausmann, R., and D. Rodrik, 2003, "Economic Development as Self-Discovery," *Journal of Development Economics*, Vol. 72, No. 2.

Heckscher, E., 1919, "The Effects of Foreign Trade on the Distribution of Income," *Economisk Tidskrift*, Vol. 21, pp. 497–512.

Helpman, E., and P. Krugman, 1985, *Market Structure and Foreign Trade* (Cambridge, MA: MIT Press).

Henderson, J., P. Dicken, M. Hess, N. Coe, and H. Wai-Chung Yeung, 2002, "Global Production Networks and the Analysis of Economic Development," *Review of International Political Economy*, Vol. 9, No. 3.

Hill, H., 1994, "The Indonesian Textiles and Garments Industries: Structure, Developments and Strategies," in *Managing Restructuring in the Textile and Garment Subsector: Examples from Asia*, ed. S. D. Meyanathan (Washington, D.C.: World Bank).

Hirschman, A. O., 1958, *The Strategy of Economic Development* (New Haven, CT: Yale University Press).

Hummels, D., 2001, "Time as a Trade Barrier," draft, Purdue University, Indiana.

Iarossi, G., 2006, *The Power of Survey Design* (Washington D.C.: World Bank).

Irwin, D. A., 2005, *Free Trade under Fire* (Princeton, NJ: Princeton University Press).

Islam, S., 1994, "Foreign Investment Effects on Balance of Payments: A Bangladesh Case Study," *Asian Survey*, Vol. 34, No. 4.

Joint Apparel Associations Forum (JAAF), 2007, http://www.jaafsl.com/.

Kabeer, N., 2000, *The Power to Choose: Bangladeshi Women and Labour Market Decisions in London and Dhaka* (London: Verso).

Kaplinsky, R., and M. Morris, 2002, "A Handbook for Value Chain Research," http://.ids.ac.uk.

Kathuria, S., and A. Bhardwaj, 1998, "Export Quotas and Policy Constraints in the Indian Textile and Garment Industries," World Bank Policy Research Working Paper No. 2012, Washington, D. C.

Keesing, D., and M. Wolf, 1980, *Textile Quotas against Developing Countries* (London: Trade Policy Research Centre).

Kelegama, S., and R. Epaarachchi, 2002, "Garment Industry in Sri Lanka" in ed. G. Joshi, "Garment Industry in South Asia: Rags or Riches? Competitiveness, Productivity and Job Quality in the post-MFA environment," South Asia Multidisciplinary Advisory Team (SAAT), International Labor Organization, New Delhi.

Kelegama, S., 2005, "Ready-Made Garment Industry in Sri Lanka: Preparing to Face the Global Challenges," *Asia Pacific Trade and Investment Review*, Vol. 1, No 1.

———, and R. Epaarachchi, 2002, "Garment Industry in Sri Lanka" in *Garment Industry in South Asia: Rags or Riches? Competitiveness, Productivity and Job Quality in the Post-MFA Environment*, ed. G. Joshi, South Asia Multidisciplinary Advisory Team (SAAT), International Labor Organization, New Delhi.

Khan, F. C., 2000, "A Decade of Trade Liberalization: How has Domestic Industry Fared in Bangladesh?" *Journal of Bangladesh Studies*, Vol.1, No. 2.

Khan, S. R., 2007, "WTO, IMF and the Closing of Development Policy Space for Low-Income countries: A Case for Neo-Developmentalism," *Third World Quarterly*, Vol. 28, No. 6.

a

————, and S. Kazmi, 2008, "Value Chains in the Informal Sector: Income Shares of Home-Based Sub-Contracted Workers in Pakistan," *International Review of Applied Economics*, Vol. 22, No. 3.

————, C. Bilginsoy, and M. S. Alam, 1997, "Dynamic Efficiencies of Industrialization and Economic Growth," *Economia Internationale*, Vol. 50, No. 1.

————, M. S. Qureshi, S. R. Khan, and M. A. Khwaja, 2003, "The Costs and Benefits of Compliance with International Environmental Standards," in *Sustainable Development and Southern Realities: Past and Future in South Asia* (Karachi: City Press).

Krishna, K., and L. Tan, 1998, *Rags and Riches: Implementing Apparel Quotas under the Multi-Fibre Arrangement* (Ann Arbor: University of Michigan Press).

Krishna, P., 2005, "The Economics of Preferential Trade Agreements," in, *Handbook of International Trade*, Vol. II, eds. E. K. Choi and J. Hartigan (Malden, MA: Blackwell).

Krugman, P., 1980, "Scale Economies, Product Differentiation, and the Pattern of Trade," *American Economic Review*, Vol. 70, No. 5.

————, 1991, *Geography and Trade* (Cambridge, MA: MIT Press).

Kuruppu, R. U., 2006, *Facets of the Clothing Industry in Sri Lanka* (Nugegoda, Sri Lanka: Modern Book Co.).

Leontief, W., 1954, "Domestic Production and Foreign Trade: The American Capital Position Reexamined," *Economia Internazionale*, Vol. 7, pp. 3–32 (reprint).

————, 1956, "Factor Proportions and the Structure of American Trade: Further Theoretical and Empirical Analysis," *Review of Economics and Statistics*, Vol. 48, No. 2.

Levinsohn, J., A. V. Deardorff, and R. M. Stern, 1995, *New Directions in Trade Theory* (Ann Arbor: University of Michigan Press).

Lezama, M., B. Webber, and C. Dagher, 2004, "Sourcing Practices in the Apparel Industry, Post 2004: Implication for Commonwealth Developing Countries," seminar paper, Commonwealth Secretariat, London, United Kingdom.

Linder, S. B., 1961, *An Essay on Trade and Transformation* (New York: Wiley).

Manjur, A., 2002, "Garment Industry in Pakistan," in *Garment Industry in South Asia: Rags or Riches? Competitiveness, Productivity and Job Quality in the Post-MFA Environment*, ed. G. Joshi, South Asia Multidisciplinary Advisory Team (SAAT), International Labor Organization, New Delhi.

Matson, J., 1990, "Deindustrialization or Peripheralization? The Case of Cotton Textiles in India, 1750–1950," in *South Asia and World Capitalism* (Delhi: Oxford University Press).

Mavroidis, P. C., 2005, "Do Not Ask Too Many Questions: The Institutional Arrangements for Accommodating Regional Integration within the WTO," in *Handbook of International Trade*, Vol. II, eds. E. K. Choi and J. Hartigan (Malden, MA: Blackwell).

McKinsey & Company, 2001, *India: The Growth Imperative* (New Delhi: McKinsey).

Meyanathan, S. D., and J. Ahmed, 1994, "Managing Restructuring in the Textile and Garment Subsector: An Overview," in ed. S. D. Meyanathan, *Managing Restructuring in the Textile and Garment Subsector*, (Washington D. C.: World Bank, Economic Development Institute).

Mlachila, M., and Y. Yang, 2004, "The End of Textile Quotas: A Case Study of the Impact on Bangladesh," IMF Working Paper 04/108, Policy Development and Review Department, Washington, D. C., http://www.imf.org/external/pubs/ft/wp/2004/wp04108.pdf.

Myrdal, G., 1957, *Economic Theory and Underdeveloped Regions* (London: Duckworth).

Nadvi, K., 1999, "The Response of Pakistan's Surgical Instrument Cluster to Global Quality Pressure," eds. K. Nadvi and H. Schmitz, special issue of *World Development on Clustering and Industrialization*, Vol. 27, No. 9.

———, and G. Halder, 2002, "Local Clusters in Global Value Chains: Exploring Dynamic Linkages between Germany and Pakistan," Institute of Development Studies, Working Paper No. 152.

———, and H. Schmitz, 1994, "Industrial Clusters in Less Developed Countries: A Review of Experiences and Research Agenda," Institute of Development Studies, University of Sussex, Discussion Paper No. 339, Brighton, Sussex.

Nepal Rastra Bank (NRB), *Quarterly Economic Bulletin*, Kathmandu, Nepal, various issues.

Nordas, H. K., 2004, "The Global Textile and Clothing Industry and Clothing," WTO Discussion Paper No. 5, Geneva.

Nusrat, J., 2005, "Global Trading Environment: Opportunities & Challenges for Pakistan," Government of Pakistan, Export Promotion Bureau, TESM Directorate, Islamabad.

Ocampo, J. A., 1986, "New Developments in Trade Theory and LDCs," *Journal of Development Economics*, Vol. 22, No. 1.

OECD, Organisation for Economic Co-operation and Development, 2004, "A New World Map in Textiles and Clothing: Adjusting to Change," OECD Policy Brief, http://www.oecd.org/dataoecd/43/14/33824605.pdf.

Office of Textile and Apparel (OTEXA), Department of Commerce, Washington, D. C., www.otexa.ita.doc.gov.

Ohlin, B., 1933, *Interregional and International Trade* (Cambridge, MA: Harvard University Press).

Okhla Garment and Textile Cluster, 2007, *OGTC Newsletter*, Vol. 5, New Delhi.

———, 2007, *OGTC Newsletter*, Vol. 6, New Delhi.

Ozawa, T., 2005, *Institutions, Industrial Upgrading, and Economic Performance in Japan—The "Flying-Geese" Paradigm of Catch-Up Growth* (Northampton, MA: Edward Elgar).

Panthaki, M. K., 2003, "Transaction Costs in Garment Industry I & II," http/www.express textile.com/20030918/edit02/shtml.

Porter, M., 1990, *The Competitive Advantage of Nations* (New York: Free Press).

Prebish, R., 1950, *The Economic Development of Latin America and its Principal Problems* (New York: United Nations).

Preetha, M. S., 2007, "Textile Exporters seek more support," *Hindu*, August 5.

Quasem, A. S. M., 2002, "Adding Value: Building Value-Addition Alliances. Backward Linkages in the Textile and Clothing Sector of Bangladesh," paper presented at the 2002 Executive Forum on National Export Strategies, Managing Competitive Advantage: The Values of National Strategy, Montreux, Switzerland, September, 25–28, 2002.

Rahman, S., 2004, "Global Shift: Bangladesh Garment Industry in Perspective," *Asian Affairs*, Vol. 26, No. 1.

Raikes, P., M. F. Jensen, and S. Ponte, 2000, "Global Commodity Chain Analysis and the French Filière Approach: Comparison and Critique," *Economy and Society*, Vol. 29, No. 3.

Ramaswamy, K. V., and G. Gereffi, 2000, "India's Apparel Exports: The Challenge of Global Markets," *Developing Economies*, Vol. 38, No. 2.

Rhee, Y. W., 1990, "Catalyst Model of Development: Lessons from Bangladesh's Success with Garment Exports," *World Development*, Vol. 18, No. 2.

Ricardo, D., 1962, *The Principles of Political Economy and Taxation* (London: Dent).

Rock, M. T., 1995, "Thai Industrial Policy: How Irrelevant Was It to Export Success?" *Journal of Industrial Development*, Vol. 7, No. 5.

Rodrik, D., 2006, "What's So Special about China's Exports?" National Bureau of Economic Research, Working Paper No. 11947, Boston, MA.

———, 2008, "Second Best Institutions," *American Economic Review*, Vol. 98, No. 2.

Rothermund, D., 1993, *An Economic History of India: From Pre-Colonial Times to 1991* (London: Routledge).

RoyChowdhury, S., 1995, "Political Economy of India's Textile Industry: The Case of Maharashtra, 1984–1989," *Pacific Affairs*, Vol. 68, No. 2.

Saxonhouse, G. R., 2005, "How Japan First Began to Export Machine-Made Manufactures to East Asia," *Japanese Economic Review*, Vol. 56, No. 4.

Schmitz, H., 1997, "Collective Efficiency and Increasing Returns," Institute of Development Studies Working Paper No. 152.

———, 2006, "Learning and Earning in Global Garment and Footwear Chains," *European Journal of Development Studies*, Vol. 18, No. 4.

Schumpeter, J. A., 1934, *Theory of Economic Development* (Cambridge, MA: Harvard University Press).

Shakya, B. M., 2005, "Analysis of Export Structure and Market Access Barriers to Nepal's Apparel Trade," a study report prepared for the Garment Association Nepal (GAN), under the grant assistance of International Trade Centre (ITC), Geneva.

Siegmann, K. A., 2005, "The Agreement on Textiles and Clothing: Potential Effects on Gendered Employment in Pakistan," International Labour Review, Vol. 144, No. 4.

Smith, A., 1973, *An Inquiry into the Nature and Causes of the Wealth of Nations* (New York: Modern Library).

Smith, D. A., 1996, "Going South: Global Restructuring and Garment Production in Three East Asian Cases," *Asian Perspective*, Vol. 20, No. 2.

South Asia Watch for Trade, Economics and Environment (SAWTEE) and Action Aid Nepal (AAN), 2007, "Impact of Textiles and Clothing Quota Phase Out on Nepal: A Study from Human Development Perspective," Kathmandu, Nepal, http://www.sawtee.org/pdf/T&C%20Book.pdf.

Uchikawa, S., 1999, *Indian Textile Industry—State Policy, Liberalization and Growth* (New Delhi: Manohar Publications).

UNCTAD, 2004, "The Least Developed Countries Report," United Nations Conference on Trade and Development, Geneva.

UNDP, 2006, "Adjusting to a New Era for Textile and Clothing," chapter 4 in Asia *Pacific Human Development Report 2006: Trade on Human Terms*, Colombo Regional Center, Sri Lanka, http://www.undprcc.lk/aphdr2006.

United Nations, 2007, UN TRAINS data, www.untrains.com.

United States International Trade Commission (USITC), 2004, "Textiles and Apparel: Assessment of the Competitiveness of Certain Foreign suppliers to the U.S. Market," a public version of the report, publication 3671, submitted to the United States Trade Representative, Washington, D.C., June 30, 2003.

Verma, S., 2002, "Export Competitiveness of Indian Textile and Garment Industry," India and Economic Cooperation in South Asia (ICRIER), Working Paper No. 94, New Delhi.

Vernon, R., 1966, "International Investment and International Trade in the Product Cycle," *Quarterly Journal of Economics*, Vol. 80, No. 2.

Wade, R., 1990, 2004, *Governing the Market: Economic Theory and the Role of Government in East Asian Industrialization* (Princeton, NJ: Princeton University Press).

Wallerstein, I., 1974, *The Modern World System* (New York: Academic Press).

Wickramsinghe, U., 2006, "Overcoming Supply-Side Constraints in South Asia," Discussion Paper, SWATEE (South Asia Watch on Trade, Economics and the Environment), Kathmandu, Nepal, http://www.sawtee.org/pdf/discussion%20paper_upali.pdf.

World Bank, 1995, "Bangladesh from Stabilization to Growth: A World Bank Country Study," Washington, D.C.

———, 2002, *World Development Report 2003* (New York: Oxford University Press).

———, 2004, "Textile and Clothing Policy Note: Implications for Pakistan of Abolishing Textile and Clothing Export Quotas," World Bank Development Research Group and the Trade Department, Washington, D.C.

———, 2006, "Bangladesh End of MFA Quotas: Key Issues and Strategic Options for Bangladesh Readymade Garment Industry," Poverty Reduction and Economic Management Sector Unit, South Asian Region, Washington, D. C.

———, 2006, *Doing Business in 2006* (Washington, D. C.: World Bank; New York: Oxford University Press).

World Bank/SMEDA, 2003, "Improving the Investment Climate in Pakistan," investment climate assessment, the World Bank Group in collaboration with the Small and Medium Enterprise Development Authority of the Government of Pakistan, Washington, D. C./Islamabad.

Index

The letter t following a page number denotes a table

neoclassical, 5
"new" models of, 154n13
process omission in, 3, 4
transition from classical to
neoclassical, 153n8
economies of scale, in India, 62–63
emerging economics, 156n4
entrepreneurship, 9–10, 20
Bangladeshi, 47
Indian, 33, 47, 64, 66–68, 75, 78,
80–81
Nepali, 83, 88, 91–97
Pakistani, 104–5, 109, 112
in RMG success, 64
Sri Lankan, 120–21
environmental issues. *See* compliance
issues
European Union
compliance issues and, 53, 56
Indian exports to, 40t, 58t
Nepali exports to, 84, 84t, 85t, 86t
Sri Lankan exports to, 121
exchange rate, Indian, garment exports
and, 68
Export Oriented Units, 76
contract labor regulations in, 78
in India, 139
Export Processing Zone in Pakistan, 109
export success
defined, 20–21
government role in, 9
historical factors in, 10
local-foreign partnerships and, 11–12
policy impacts, 10–11
political factors in, 10
processes accounting for, 3–4
public-private partnerships and, 11
research question and conceptual
framework for, 3–4, 21–24
themes in, 9–12

F
factor endowment model, 5
Faisalabad Garment City, 110

family ties. *See* social capital
flying geese paradigm, 26, 36, 156n2
foreign direct investment
in India, 67, 77
constraints on, 80–81
Indian shortage of, 140
in Sri Lanka, 169n6
Foreign Trade Policy of 2004 (India),
75, 139
free-trade agreements, Nepali RMG
sector and, 96
free-trade zones, Sri Lankan, 120

G
Gap stores, compliance issues and, 73
Garment Association of Nepal, 92
garment cities, concept of, 109–10
Pakistani, 140
garment processing zone, Nepali need
for, 92, 96
General Agreement on Trade and
Tariffs, 34
Gil Garments, 120
global value chains, 8–9
characteristics of, 8–9
defined, 8
producer versus buyer-driven, 8–9
Globe Managements, 105, 115,
167n15
Gokaldas Images, 63–64
supply-chain partnerships of, 71–72
government
Bangladesh RMG sector
and, 49, 55
business attitudes toward, 138
export incentives and, 9
Indian RMG sector and, 74–75
Nepali RMG sector and, 88–89,
92–93, 96
Pakistani RMG sector and, 106–11,
110–11, 116–17
Sri Lankan RMG sector and,
126–28
See also industrial policies

DATE DUE	RETURNED